Celebrity Lights II

Celebrity Lights II

A Collection of Favourite Recipes from Celebrity Women
in Support of Breast Cancer Research

Celebrity Lights Foundation
Nanaimo, British Columbia, Canada

WOMEN *to* WOMEN
A Gift of Hope

Canadian Cataloguing in Publication Data

Main entry under title:
    Celebrity Lights II

Includes index.
ISBN 0-9681159-1-8

    1. Cookery. I. Dash, Donna II. Mason, Karen, 1962–
III. Celebrity Lights Foundation

TX714.C445 1998   641.5   C98-901005-8

Project Co-ordinator & Managing Editor	Donna Dash
Assistant Editor	Karen Mason
Graphic Designer & Illustrator	Valerie Luedke
Digital Pre-Press Coordinator/Web Author	Joanne Hogan
Proofreaders:	Adella Krall, Michelle Krall
Photographer	Kim Stallknecht
Food Stylist	Deborah Melanson
Prop Stylist	Shelley Anderson
Food Technicians	Jessica Melanson, Karen Mason, Shelley Anderson, Iola Feser

First Printing – 1998

Printed in Canada by Fleming Printing Ltd., Victoria, British Columbia
and Friesens Book Division, Altona, Manitoba, on Luna stock from
Island Paper Mills Co. Ltd., New Westminster, British Columbia.

Celebrity Lights II is dedicated to women everywhere who have lost their lives to breast cancer.

Acknowledgements

"It only takes one candle to turn darkness into day, but with the lights of many, we'll surely find a way.." These words symbolize the journey that will ultimately lead the world to a cure for breast cancer. From the haunting lyrics of Shelley Chase in a song created to launch *Celebrity Lights II*, the analogy can also be used to describe the production of this book, for it took many 'lights' to lead this project to where it is today.

Shining brightest among them are the contributing celebrities. Their gift is this beautiful and unique collection of recipes. From a variety of countries and numerous fields of endeavour, these exceptional women have something very special in common: all are extremely talented, caring individuals and all have shared a part of themselves to help with this important cause. We thank them.

To the other group of women who made this book possible, the Celebrity Lights Production Team, thank you for sharing my dream. I've always believed a good team can accomplish almost anything, and *Celebrity Lights II* reinforces that belief. With Deb's knowledge of food, Valerie's talent as a designer, Kim's expertise with a camera, Karen's help with both editing and cooking, Shelley's flair for fabrics and set decor, Jessica's skill in the kitchen, Cora's sound legal advice and Carrie's advertising experience, how could we go wrong? Add to that the organizational abilities of Lynn and the enthusiasm of Adella and Michelle in helping to plan our launch, and we really do have the complete "Recipe for Success". A big hug to each of you for your commitment. You are not only the most gifted women I know, but also my dearest friends.
(See a photo of this incredible team on page 165.)

To Deborah Melanson, President of the Celebrity Lights Foundation, you are the greatest! To take on this role, with your extremely busy schedule, is an example of the kind of woman you are, always willing to go that extra mile to help others.

A very special thanks to our corporate sponsors – Pat Lumsden and the Royal Bank of Canada, Thomas Gemma, Susan Radui and their associates at The Bay, Wayne Stremel of Canada Post, and Tom Cochrane of First Strike Consulting. We also look forward to Overwaitea Foods' and Don Kraushar's continued support, along with the dozens of stores and services that helped sell the first book, which I just know will stay involved again this time. It is the combined effort of so many retailers and corporate donors that has made this project financially feasible.

Edith Wharton's quote: "There are two ways of spreading light: to be the candle or the mirror that reflects it" sums up the importance of our corporate supporters. They are the 'candles' that provided the initial light, so that others could enjoy the reflection. With the help of many and the benefit of the Internet, there are now literally hundreds and thousands of 'mirrors' reflecting Celebrity Lights in different parts of the world.

Who would have guessed two years ago when we started this fund-raising initiative that it would be so exciting and so rewarding. It seems the more you give to Celebrity Lights, the more it radiates back in the form of friendships, personal fulfillment and empowerment.

I thank my family for believing in me and for their perseverance in helping to sell books. Mom, I also appreciate the many desserts you baked! Barry, thank you for putting up with my passion for this project. Ron, Hilary and Oliver, you are my inspiration.

To all the families of the production team members, thank you for your continued support and encouragement.

Last, but not least, 'thank you' to everyone for purchasing books and sharing this gift in the hope that some day soon breast cancer will be beaten.

Sincerely

Donna Dash

Donna Dash
Managing Editor & Project Co-ordinator

Introduction

Last year, while traveling to Spokane, I met a most remarkable woman. Connie, a three-time breast cancer survivor, was undergoing a radical and experimental therapy for yet another cancer discovered in her hip. As we spoke, her profound courage and enthusiasm for life startled me. Connie saw all that was beautiful, thirsted for living and treasured each day as a lovely gift. Her excitement for the *Celebrity Lights* project echoed in my ears as we parted paths.

While attending my friend's Bar Mitzvah in California, I met a young woman who was just diagnosed with a lump in her breast and was waiting for her results. As we sat at our table offering support to Susan, five out of seven women identified that they, their moms or sisters had fallen victim to this horrific disease.

I shared with them the *Celebrity Lights* book, a little cookbook with a lot of hope. I asked them to carry the flame into California to help support our project and to give the gift of hope to women everywhere.

As the president of the Celebrity Lights Foundation, I am still saddened by the vast numbers of women I meet who are affected by breast cancer.

Celebrity Lights was originally envisioned as a gift of hope from women to women and, through this second edition, we hope to keep the candle glowing. With your help and support for this project, we can continue to search for the light at the end of the tunnel.

A short time before our press deadline, cancer took the talented and beautiful Shari Lewis away much too soon. This children's advocate, actor, puppeteer and entertainer shared her light with a legion of children worldwide.

Before she passed away, Shari expressed a wish to participate in the Celebrity Lights project, and we are honoured to include her recipe in this book in a special category at the end, suitably named "Shining Light."

Celebrity Lights II is being dedicated specially to Linda McCartney, who suffered not only a private battle with this disease, but a public one. As a photographer, Linda held dear the "light" and its ability to cast a glow of warmth, where none was apparent before. Linda's light reached us; we were touched by her career, her life and her family's loss. For Linda, Shari and others, *Celebrity Lights II* is a tribute to all women whose candles have been dimmed before their time.

I thank Donna Dash, editor and project coordinator for her vision, passion and dedication to this book. Without Donna's dream, our project would not exist. A heartfelt thank you to the production team, my family and my co-workers for their support and enthusiasm for this little book with a whole lot of impact... we have just begun.

Deborah Melanson

Deborah Melanson
President
Celebrity Lights Foundation
Nanaimo, British Columbia, Canada
1998

Table of Contents

The Book

The Lights

Morning Light

Sunlight

11

Candlelight

Firelight

Shining Light

Guiding Light

The Project

About the Recipes

Our "lights" recipe categories were created to reflect the theme of Celebrity Lights. With a very few exceptions, they are certainly not definitive. For example, Barbara Bush's Mushroom Quiche makes a hearty brunch dish in the "Morning Light" category. However, it would be an equally popular selection for lunch ("Sunlight") or even a light supper ("Twilight"). Feel free to move these recipes, like candles, to create new lights among your own traditions.

Our "light" theme is also strictly aesthetic, not medical or scientific. While net proceeds from sales of *Celebrity Lights II* will go to support breast cancer research, this book is not a diet or a collection of recipes assembled for the prevention or treatment of any disease, including breast cancer. Questions about diet and health, especially with respect to illness, should be directed to a physician. Nor are the recipes contained in this book necessarily "light" insofar as fat or carbohydrate content. Celebrity Lights Foundation is publishing *Celebrity Lights II* for the purpose of creating awareness and raising money for breast cancer research.

Some of these recipes arrived handwritten and some arrived typeset on the latest digital equipment. Regardless of how they came, we have made every effort to accurately and faithfully reproduce them in every detail. In some submissions, measurements have been estimated, because many old family favourites never had quantities written down. So if you find that a particular measure doesn't work for you, adjust the quantity and try again. After all, that's usually how our own most treasured recipes evolve.

Abbreviations are used for most measurements throughout *Celebrity Lights II* to conserve space and improve ease of reading. These are the standard abbreviations:

tsp	teaspoon	oz	ounce
tbsp	tablespoon	lb	pound
pkg	package	qt	quart

Metric Conversions

All measurements in *Celebrity Lights II* are Imperial and/or conventional. Standard metric equivalents are provided below.

Metric measures do not always exactly equal conventional measures, so in some cases, metrics have been rounded up or down (e.g., 1/4 cup = 56.8 millilitres, rounded down to a standard 50 millilitres). Exact metric measures are shown in brackets where numbers have been rounded up or down by more than 5.

The benchmark for this book is 1 cup (8 fluid ounces or 16 tablespoons) = 250 millilitres.

Liquid

1/4 teaspoon	1 millilitre
1/2 teaspoon	2 millilitres
1 teaspoon	5 millilitres
1-1/2 teaspoons	7 millilitres
2 teaspoons	10 millilitres (9.4)
1 tablespoon	15 millilitres (14.2)
1/4 cup (4 tbsp)	50 millilitres (56.8)
1/3 cup (5-1/3 tbsp)	75 millilitres
1/2 cup (8 tbsp)	125 millilitres (113.6)
2/3 cup	150 millilitres
3/4 cup (12 tbsp)	175 millilitres
1 cup (16 tbsp)	250 millilitres (227.2)
4 cups (1 quart)	900 millilitres (908.8)
4-1/2 cups	1000 millilitres, 1 litre (1022.4)

Weight

1 ounce	30 grams
1-1/2 ounces	45 grams
2 ounces	55 grams
3 ounces	85 grams
4 ounces	125 grams (113.4)
5 ounces	140 grams
6 ounces	170 grams
7 ounces	200 grams
8 ounces	250 grams (226.8)
10 ounces	280 grams
16 ounces	500 grams (453.6)
32 ounces	900 grams (907.2)
35 ounces	1000 grams, 1 kilogram (992.2)

Pans

8-inch x 2-inch round	20 cm x 5 cm
9-inch x 2-inch round	22 cm x 5 cm
8-inch by 8-inch	20 cm x 20 cm
9-inch by 9-inch	22 cm x 22 cm
9-inch x 13-inch	22 cm x 33 cm

Temperatures (all degrees)

Fahrenheit	Celsius	Fahrenheit	Celsius
175	80	350	180
200	100	375	190
225	110	400	200
250	120	425	220
275	140	450	230
300	150	475	240
325	160	500	260

The future belongs to those who believe

in the beauty of their dreams.

Eleanor Roosevelt

Morning Light

Favourites for breakfasts, brunches and coffee-breaks

Breakfast Wrap & Go!

"I went to university in Texas on a track scholarship and love all Mexican style foods like this easy to make breakfast burrito!"

2 large flour
    tortilla shells

olive oil

4 eggs

1 tbsp milk

3/4 cup chopped
    cooked ham

3/4 cup mushrooms

1/2 cup shredded
    mozzarella cheese

salt and pepper to taste

1 Romano tomato
    chopped

Heat skillet lightly coated with olive oil. Whisk together eggs, milk, salt and pepper, and cook for one minute. Add chopped ham, mushrooms and cook until tender. Heat tortillas. Place half mixture in middle of each tortilla, sprinkle with cheese and diced tomatoes and fold burrito style.

Serve with salsa if desired.

Charmaine Crooks

Five-Time Olympian, Silver Medallist, TV Host, Producer and Creator of "No Laughing Matter™" fund raiser for breast cancer research
Vancouver, British Columbia, Canada

"Projects such as this cookbook are contributing in a positive way to raise awareness of breast cancer. All women are inspired by the strength, hope and determination often shown by women battling this disease. May we 'never give up' in our hopes for a cure!"

18

WOMEN *to* WOMEN
A Gift of Hope

Apfezkratze

"This recipe came from my grandmother and we all love it!!! It can also be eaten with your favourite yogurt."

3 eggs	3 medium apples
1/2 cup milk	Cinnamon
1 cup flour	Sugar
Dash of salt	

Separate egg white from yolk. Beat the egg whites until stiff.

In a separate bowl – add flour, milk and salt to egg yolks. Mix well. Fold egg whites into the batter.

Peel apples and cut into 4 quarters. Then cut each quarter into thin slices and fold in to batter.

In a pan put butter, margarine or Pam and batter. Cook like a pancake on medium heat. Once light brown on one side turn pancake over. Don't worry if it breaks, you scramble up the whole thing anyway. Cook until apples become soft.

Mix cinnamon and sugar to your liking and sprinkle over apfezkratze.

Serves 3.

Sarah Young

Denise Brown

Founder, Nicole Brown Simpson Charitable Foundation
Laguna Beach, California, U.S.A.

"Thank you so much for letting me be a part of your Celebrity Lights II Cookbook. *Breast Cancer can affect any one of us. It can be a very scary situation for a woman to be in. We have to support one another and be there for one another."*

WOMEN *to* WOMEN
A Gift of Hope

Easy, Creamy Scrambled Eggs

"Brunch is my favourite food occasion. Whenever it's my turn to make it, I rely on the delicious recipes from our food writers at *Homemaker's Magazine*. This one for 'Easy, Creamy Scrambled Eggs' comes from Jan Main."

3 tbsp butter

1/2 lb mushrooms, sliced

6 green onions, chopped

16 large eggs, beaten

2 tbsp all-purpose flour

2 cups milk

1 cup shredded Swiss cheese (1/4 lb)

1/2 tsp salt

1/4 tsp each pepper and nutmeg

Herbed Crumb Topping

1/4 cup melted butter

2 cups fresh breadcrumbs

2 tbsp chopped fresh parsley

1/2 tsp dried thyme

WOMEN *to* WOMEN

A Gift of Hope

In large skillet, melt 1 Tbsp of the butter over medium heat. Add mushrooms and onions; cook 5 minutes, until softened. Add eggs; cook stirring 15 to 20 minutes or until eggs are just set. Remove from heat. In medium saucepan, melt remaining butter over medium heat. Stir in flour; cook, stirring, 2 to 3 minutes or until flour begins to turn pale brown. Remove saucepan from heat; gradually whisk in milk. Return to heat; cook, whisking constantly, 5 minutes, or until sauce thickens. Whisk in cheese, salt, pepper and nutmeg until cheese melts. Pour sauce over eggs; fold in until well combined. Spoon egg mixture into buttered 13" X 9" baking dish; set aside.

Herbed Crumb Topping

In small bowl, combine melted butter, bread crumbs, parsley and thyme. Sprinkle evenly over egg mixture. Refrigerate, covered, up to 12 hours. To serve, bake, uncovered, in 350°F oven 30 minutes or until heated through. Serve at once.

Sally Armstrong

Editor-in-Chief,
Homemaker's Magazine
Toronto, Ontario, Canada

"To all the wonderful women who have made a difference in the fight against breast cancer"

Coleen Christie

Host/Reporter,
Vancouver Television
Vancouver, British Columbia,
Canada

Coleen's Fluffy Blueberry Pancakes

3 egg yolks

1 1/2 cups buttermilk

1 tsp baking soda

1 1/4 cups unsifted all
purpose flour

2 tsp sugar

1 tsp baking powder

1/2 tsp salt

3 tbsp melted butter

1/2 tsp vanilla

3 egg whites

1/2 to 3/4 cup
blueberries*

Beat egg yolks well. Stir buttermilk and soda together and add vanilla. Stir into egg yolks. Sift flour with sugar, baking powder and salt and add to egg and buttermilk mixture. Add butter. Beat egg whites to stiff peaks. Fold into batter. Add 1/2 to 3/4 cup fresh or frozen blueberries.

Pour from tablespoon onto greased hot griddle. Flip when bubbles form at edges. Serve with butter and maple syrup.

Makes 14 to 16 pancakes.

*May substitute bananas or your favourite fruit
for the blueberries.

WOMEN to WOMEN
A Gift of Hope

Mushroom Quiche

3 tbsp margarine

1 1/4 lbs mushrooms, sliced

3 green onions, minced

1 clove garlic, minced

3 shallots, minced

1 3/4 tsp oregano

1 3/4 tsp basil

1 1/4 tsp salt

3/4 tsp marjoram

1/4 tsp black pepper

1/4 tsp thyme

1/2 tsp dry mustard

4 eggs

3/4 cup milk

1 unbaked 9" pie crust

Preheat oven to 375°F. Melt butter in large skillet over medium heat. Sauté mushrooms, onions, garlic and shallots together. Stir in seasonings, cook for 2 minutes until liquid is evaporated. Let cool five minutes. In medium size bowl combine eggs with milk and beat well. Stir in mushroom mixture and pour into pie crust. Bake until filling is puffed, set and starting to brown, about 35 to 45 minutes.

Serves 6.

Barbara Bush

Former First Lady of the United States of America
Houston, Texas, U.S.A.

"Best wishes for success with your effort."

WOMEN to WOMEN
A Gift of Hope

Calvin Fehr

Hon. Janice MacKinnon

History Professor,
Minister of Economic and
Co-operative Development
Province of Saskatchewan
Regina, Saskatchewan, Canada

"I appreciate being asked to join in
this important endeavour. My best
wishes for every success."

Mushroom and
Ham Tarts

2 cups finely chopped
   mushrooms

1/2 cup chopped onion

1/4 cup butter

1 cup minced lean
   cooked ham

1 /2 cup grated
   Swiss cheese

1/4 snipped fresh dill or
   3/4 tsp dried dill weed

pepper

16 small unbaked
   tart shells

Add mushrooms and onion to heated butter in
skillet. Cover and cook over medium-low heat
until very tender, 8 to 10 minutes. Uncover
and continue cooking until accumulated liquid
evaporates and mixture is just moist, 3 to
4 minutes, stirring often. Remove from heat.
Stir in ham, cheese and dill. Season generously
with pepper. Fill tart shells with mixture, dividing
evenly. Bake at 425°F until pastry is golden and
filling appears firm on top, 10 to 15 minutes.

WOMEN *to* WOMEN
A Gift of Hope

Rita's Tea Room Cinnamon Rolls

8 cups flour

1/2 cup sugar

6 tbsp baking powder

1 tsp salt

1 lb shortening

3 – 3 1/2 cups water

1 cup soft margarine

1 tbsp cinnamon

2 cups brown sugar

Mix flour, sugar, baking powder and salt. Cut in 1 lb shortening with pastry blender until mixed. Add water until mixture forms a stiff ball. Roll out into a large rectangle (1/8" thick) on well floured counter. If you have a small working surface, divide dough into two equal pieces. Spread a thin layer of margarine over entire surface.

Combine brown sugar and cinnamon and mix well. Spread brown sugar mixture on buttered dough.

Starting from bottom, left to right, roll dough up.

Cut into 1/2" pieces. Place on a lightly greased cookie sheet. Pinch end of each cinnamon roll.

Bake at 350°F for 15 to 20 minutes. Remove; let cool on cookie sheet.

Rita MacNeil

Singer/Songwriter
Cape Breton, Nova Scotia, Canada

"This is an important and worthy cause. Wishing you success with this fund raising campaign."

Rita's Tea Room Cinnamon Rolls are pictured on page 99.

WOMEN to WOMEN
A Gift of Hope

Komishbroit (Jewish Biscotti)

"These cookies have everything: they remind me of my mother, they're easy and forgiving, they're not fattening, and they're delicious."

3 eggs

1 cup packed brown sugar

1 cup oil

3 cups flour

1 1/2 tsp baking soda

1 1/2 tsp baking powder

1 cup coarsely chopped nuts (almonds, filberts, Brazil)

1 tsp vanilla flavouring

1 tsp almond flavouring

cinnamon

Beat eggs and sugar until combined. Add oil and beat until incorporated. Add flour and everything else gradually until dough holds together and is soft but not sticky. Divide dough into three equal pieces.

WOMEN *to* WOMEN
A Gift of Hope

Pat dough into rectangle about 5" x 10". Sprinkle with cinnamon. Roll up like a jelly roll. Place on cookie sheet and pat it into a roll about 3" x 12". Repeat with two remaining pieces of dough.

Bake at 350°F until lightly browned, about 30 minutes.

Slip rolls onto a cutting board and let cool, about 2 to 3 minutes. Slice about half inch thick. Place the slices, cut side down on cookie sheet. Reduce oven temperature to 275°F and bake until pleasantly brown.

Makes about 50 cookies.

Dian Nusgart Cohen, C.M., LL.D

Economic Communications Consultant
Ayer's Cliff, Quebec, Canada

"Your volunteer effort with Celebrity Lights is a model for everyone who wants to make a difference. Your story, as well as the story of the Corporate Fund for Breast Cancer Research goes to the heart of what dedicated volunteers can do."

3 Cs (Cranberries, Coconut, Cherries)

"Best use of Arctic berries. Use lowbush cranberries grown on the tundra which have a distinctive tart taste. May be substituted with chopped store bought cranberries.

"'Best therapeutic time for thinking is when you're berry picking.'

"Ingredients are easy to source. Good for kids. Healthy. Easy cake for any occasion."

2 1/2 cups all purpose flour

1/2 tsp salt

2 tsp baking powder

1/2 tsp baking soda

1 tsp cinnamon

1/2 cup cooking oil

1 cup white sugar

3 eggs

1/2 cup milk

2 cups carrot, shredded

1 1/2 cups cranberries (lowbush)

1 1/3 cups coconut, unsweetened, shredded

1/2 cup maraschino cherries, chopped

1/2 cup raisins

1/2 cup pecans

1 tbsp grated orange peel

Preheat oven to 350°F. Mix cranberries, coconut, maraschino berries, raisins, pecans and grated orange peel. Set aside.

Mix together flour, salt, baking powder, baking soda and cinnamon in a mixing bowl. Set aside.

Beat eggs with sugar until smooth. Stir in milk and oil. Add carrot. Mix well and pour the entire mixture into the flour mixture. Stir. Add in the cranberries mixture. Stir.

Scrape into a greased 9" tube or bundt pan.

Bake for 50 to 60 minutes or until it begins to shrink away from sides of pan. Cool about 30 minutes before removing from pan.

Hon. Nellie J.Cournoyea

Chair and CEO of Inuvialuit Regional Corporation; Former Premier of Northwest Territories
Inuvik, Northwest Territories, Canada

Keep your face to the sunshine and

you cannot see the shadows

Helen Keller

Sunlight

Midday recipes for hot and cold lunches

WOMEN *to* WOMEN
A Gift of Hope

6-Onion Soup

"A favourite of many. Quick, delicious and mysterious!"

4 tbsp butter

2 tbsp olive oil

6 medium firm yellow onions, thinly sliced

3 large leeks (whites only) thoroughly rinsed and thinly sliced crosswise

4 large scallions, trimmed of all but 2 inches of green tops, sliced lengthwise

2 garlic cloves, minced

1/2 cup chopped shallots

4 fresh chives snipped

1/8 tsp sugar

salt and freshly ground pepper

2 tsp flour

5 cups good vegetable stock

4 cups water

1 cup fine French burgundy

1/2 tsp dried thyme

pinch of nutmeg

6 toasted French Bread rounds

1 lb Gruyere or Emmenthaler cheese, grated

WOMEN *to* WOMEN
A Gift of Hope

Heat the butter and oil in a large heavy casserole. Add onions, leeks, scallions, garlic, shallots and chives. Cover and sauté over moderate heat 5 minutes, stirring only once.

Add the sugar, salt and pepper to taste and continue cooking 30 minutes, stirring frequently until onions are very brown and reduced in bulk by at least one-half.

Add the flour, stir and cook 2 minutes longer. Add 2 cups stock, bring to boil and scrape bottom of the casserole. Add the remaining stock, the water, wine, thyme and nutmeg and return to boil, then lower heat, cover and simmer gently for 45 minutes.

Pre-heat oven to 375°F. Divide soup evenly among 6 to 8 deep individual oven proof soup bowls and place a toasted bread round in the center of each, top each with generous mound of mixed grated cheese and bake on sheet in oven for 15 minutes until cheese is golden brown.

Hon. Iona (Hardy) Campagnolo

Activist Citizen
Chancellor of University of
Northern British Columbia
Broadcaster
British Columbia, Canada

"Women supporting women have helped us 'endure' since the cave – the victories we win build our confidence toward all the other challenges we face."

3-P Soup (Pat's Pear & Parsnip Soup)

"Tasty, year round recipe. Ingredients always fresh."

4 1/2 cups chicken stock	1 onion peeled and chopped
4 cups peeled, chopped parsnips	1 1/2 tsp curry powder
1 cup peeled, chopped pears	1/4 tsp pepper
	1 bay leaf
	1 cup of 1% milk

Bring all ingredients (except milk) to a boil over high heat. Reduce heat and simmer covered, stirring often, for about 30 minutes. Discard bay leaf. Transfer batches to food processor; puree until smooth. Return to sauce pan, add milk and heat through.

Soup can be refrigerated for 2 days.

Serves 6 to 8.

Michael Bedford Photography

Hon. Pat Carney, P.C.

Senator for British Columbia
Ottawa, Ontario, Canada

"Loved the first Celebrity Lights! I wish you success with this very unique and important fund raiser for breast cancer research."

WOMEN to WOMEN
A Gift of Hope

Shirley MacLaine's Favourite Chicken Mushroom Soup

1 young chicken

4 oz mushrooms

1 clove garlic, crushed

1 tsp ground coriander

1 tsp ground peppercorns

2 pints stock from chicken liquid

1 tsp soy sauce

oil for frying

Cook chicken in water until tender, remove flesh and cut into small pieces. Reboil chicken bones about 2 hours in the same water. Strain stock. Slice mushrooms, fry crushed garlic, coriander and peppercorns in a little oil. Add mushrooms and chicken meat, including the liver. Add stock and soy sauce; simmer 10 to 15 minutes. Stir well and serve.

Serves 4.

Enjoy!

Shirley MacLaine

Actor, Author, Dancer and Singer
Beverly Hills, California, U.S.A.

WOMEN to WOMEN
A Gift of Hope

35

Chicken Soup

"This is a hearty soup which my children love, and which always makes them feel better if they're 'under the weather' – it's comfort food at its best!! A large soup pot is needed for the quantity described. Great for freezing!! Great for school lunches in the Calgary winter!!"

1 roasting chicken (5 lbs) or 2 smaller chickens	5 to 8 carrots
3 to 4 quarts of water	4 to 5 parsnips
1 tbsp of salt	1 tbsp of dried dill, or a bunch of fresh dill
6 to 8 ribs of celery with leafy tops	as many mushrooms as you want
4 medium onions	pepper to taste

Rinse the chicken; trim off excess fat. Cut the chicken into quarters and place in a large soup pot. Add the water and the salt. Cover the pot and bring to a boil. Uncover and skim off the scum from the top and discard.

Chop up the onions in a "Cuisinart"; cut celery, carrots and parsnips into bite-size pieces; slice the mushrooms. Add them all to the pot and simmer for about 1 hour, perhaps 1 1/2 hours.

Remove chicken from the pot; let cool a bit and then debone it, putting the chicken into the pot. Simmer some more. Season to taste. Enjoy!!

Chief Christine Silverberg

Chief, Calgary Police Service
Calgary, Alberta, Canada

WOMEN *to* WOMEN
A Gift of Hope

Cream of Broccoli Soup — With No Cream

1 medium onion, chopped

1 clove garlic, crushed

1 tbsp sunflower oil, or other vegetable oil

1 bay leaf

1 lb green broccoli, chopped

2 1/2 cups light vegetable stock (or broth made with vegetable or chicken bouillon)

1 small potato (for thickening)

salt and pepper

juice of 1/2 lemon

low-fat plain yogurt (or sour cream, if you're not watching calories or cholesterol)

Sauté onion and garlic in the oil with bay leaf until soft (or in saucepan sprayed with PAM) 3 to 4 minutes.

Add broccoli, potato, and stock… simmer gently, covered, 10 minutes. The broccoli should be tender but still bright green. Remove bay leaf and let cool a little.

Puree in a blender (not totally smooth). Season to taste, add lemon juice. May need reheating in clean pan before serving.

Add a dollop of yogurt just before serving. Serves 4.

Rosalyn Carter

Former First Lady of the United States of America
Atlanta, Georgia, U.S.A.

"With best wishes."

WOMEN *to* WOMEN
A Gift of Hope

Christine Lippa's Chicken Soup

"When I was growing up, my mother always made food that looked different from what my friends' mothers made. That's because we were German and my friends weren't. White bread and Alphaghetti were rare and exotic treats for me, only to be consumed at my friends' houses, away from my mother's Teutonic, watchful eye. I remember going up to Forbidden Plateau on Vancouver Island on a school ski trip when I was in elementary school and pulling out my sandwich at lunchtime in the chalet. Everyone was sitting around going through what I like to call lunchtime poker, 'I got a peanut butter and jam, whatdayou got?' 'Bologna. Whatdayou got Lippa?' Well, I had a 'Met' sandwich. 'What's that?' I knew that life would never be the same once I told them, and I was right. 'Eeewwww, Lippa's eating raw meat!!!!!!!' Actually, it was Tartare, and I loved it. However, I would have gladly given up my treasured sandwich that day in lieu of running from a beating all day on the slopes by some pretty big, xenophobic grade sixers. I didn't know how to ski when I got there that morning, but by mid afternoon, I was pretty good. When I got home that night I told my mother never to make me another Met sandwich for lunch again. She looked at me and snorted, 'Vy not? Are all ze kids jealous?'

"What has this got to do with chicken soup? Nothing. But it's a good story."

"This recipe comes from my brain. It sticks to my bones and makes my insides glow."

Day 1

1 big pot filled 3/4 with water	1 onion
1 whole frying chicken (or 2 halves, or a bunch of necks and backs)	5 large carrots
	1 parsnip
	5 stalks of celery
	1 bunch of parsley
5 to 6 cloves of garlic	a couple of bay leaves

Skin the chicken as best you can; no need to get finicky. You can leave the skin on the necks and backs – I think it's too hard to remove that stuff. Plunk the chicken into the water. Chuck in the rest of the stuff after you've washed, peeled and roughly cut it. Leave the parsley in a bunch with a string around it, it's easier to fish out after.

Bring to a boil, then simmer for a few hours (I simmer mine for 4 to 6 hours). Cool down and put the whole pot into the fridge overnight.

continued on next page

Christine Lippa

*Actor, Writer,
Stand-up Comic*
Vancouver, British Columbia,
Canada

"Nothing worthwhile is easy,
but nothing should be this hard."

Christine Lippa's
Chicken Soup —continued

Day 2

more chicken

more vegetables

optional: 1/2 to 1 cup noodles (any kind you like) or rice

Haul the pot out of the fridge and lift off the hardened fat that's formed on top with a fork and chuck it away. Pour the soup through a colander and into a large bowl. (You might need to warm it up slightly if the soup is particularly gelatinous. By the way, that's how you know you have a terrific soup, the more jello-like, the better.)

Throw out all the gak in the colander after you've strained out the broth. Return the broth to the pot and reheat. Pop in another 1/2 frying chicken (or whatever cuts you'd like, they don't have to be particularly good, ie; deboned and skinned breast). Plop in chopped carrots, celery, broccoli, onion, a couple of cloves of garlic, any other veggies you want. Bring to a boil and simmer until the chicken is cooked. Fish out the chicken, cool, pick off the meat and return it to the broth. Throw out the bones.

If you want, now is the time to add noodles or rice (remember to be careful with how much you put in, as they can soak up your entire broth, believe me, I know). Another 20 minutes and you have Chicken Noodle Soup, or Chicken Vegetable Rice Soup or Chicken Vegetable Soup, it's up to you. Add salt to taste. I like adding a few drops of something called "Maggi," a liquid seasoning (hydrolyzed vegetable protein, water and salt) that tastes terrific in soups. You can find it in the grocery store around the soya sauces, etc., or in delicatessens.

When I make this soup, I put one-serving portions into ziploc bags and freeze. This makes for a handy, quick, nutritious snack that's a lot less expensive than those dried soups in a cup from the grocery store. More importantly, you'll know exactly what's in it and boy, "vill zos kids be jealous!" Guten Appetit!

Hon. Elizabeth Witmer, M.P.P.

Minister of Health, Ontario Government
Toronto, Ontario, Canada

Sweet and Nutty Broccoli Salad

"Easy, nutritious, great for barbecues at the cottage with friends. Triples and quadruples beautifully for a crowd!"

Dressing

1 1/2 cups mayonnaise

2 tbsp wine vinegar

1 tbsp Dijon mustard

3 tbsp honey

1/2 cup raisins

Salad

2 bunches broccoli
  (tips only),
  cut in florets

1 red onion, chopped

1 cup sunflower seeds
  or pine nuts

1/4 lb bacon, cooked
  and crumbled

To make dressing, combine mayonnaise, vinegar, mustard and honey. Add raisins and let stand for at least 30 minutes. The flavours blend even better if allowed to stand, refrigerated, overnight. Just before serving, combine salad ingredients; toss with dressing, so the dressing lightly coats broccoli, saving any extra dressing for another use.

Serves 8.

WOMEN *to* WOMEN
A Gift of Hope

Tabbouli Salad

2 bunches green onions,
  chopped (do not use
  green tops)

3 bunches parsley
  (use leaves only)

1 bunch fresh mint
  (or 3 tsp dried mint)

3 or 4 large fresh
  tomatoes –
  diced or chopped

1/4 cup cracked wheat
  (Bulgar)

1/2 cup olive oil

lemon juice to taste –
  at least 1/2 cup

salt and pepper to taste

Marlo Thomas

Actress, Writer
New York, New York, U.S.A.

"Good luck with the book!"

Soak wheat in water to cover, squeeze dry in clean tea towel, 10 to 15 minutes. Meanwhile, soak parsley and mint in salt water for a few minutes. Rinse well under running water, pat dry in tea towel. Remove parsley leaves, pulling them off into tiny "flowerettes", also remove mint leaves from stems.

Put bulgar in large bowl, add onions, parsley, mint and tomatoes. Stir in lemon juice, salt and pepper. Let stand in refrigerator for 1/2 hour to allow flavours to blend. Add oil just before serving. Serve on Romaine lettuce leaves.

All above ingredients my be adjusted to your own taste. If you want a tangier taste, add more lemon juice, but start with the above amounts.

Tabbouli Salad is pictured on page 100.

WOMEN *to* WOMEN
A Gift of Hope

Woman must be the pioneer in this
turning inward for strength.
In a sense she has always been the pioneer.

Anne Morrow Lindbergh

Tea Lights

Sweet afternoon delights

Calla Lilies

"These are simple to make, unusual and delicious. My mother got the recipe in the Annapolis Valley in the thirties. Perfect for afternoon tea."

Dough

2 eggs	1 tsp baking powder
1/2 cup sugar	pinch salt
1/2 cup flour	

Filling

1/2 cup whipping cream	1/4 tsp vanilla
1/2 tsp sugar	grape jelly

Preheat oven to 400°F.

Beat the eggs and gradually add the sugar. Add the flour, baking powder and salt and mix thoroughly. The dough will be runny.

Drop the dough, 1 tsp at a time, onto a greased cookie sheet. (They spread, so leave room).

WOMEN to WOMEN
A Gift of Hope

Bake in a 400°F oven until golden and top springs back when touched (5 to 8 minutes). Take from oven one at a time with pancake flipper. Pinch one end of each circle together to form a calla lily shape. Cool on rack. The cookies may be made ahead of time to this stage.

Whip cream and sweeten with 1/2 tsp of sugar and 1/4 tsp vanilla, or to taste. Put a "tongue" of grape jelly at the wide end of the lily running towards centre, fill centre with a blob of whipped cream.

Serve soon after filling.

Makes approximately 1 dozen.

Andrew MacNaughton

Margaret Atwood

Author
Toronto, Ontario, Canada

Lace Cookies

"Lace cookies are served alone or with fresh peach ice cream at the ranch. They're also perfect for that special tea or brunch."

1/3 cup flour
1/2 cup coconut
1/4 cup Karo Syrup (red or blue label)

1/4 cup brown sugar firmly packed
1/4 cup margarine
1/2 tsp vanilla

Mix flour with coconut. Mix Karo Syrup, sugar and margarine until well blended. Cook over medium heat stirring constantly. Remove from heat and stir in vanilla. Gradually blend in flour mixture.

Drop by teaspoonfuls 3" to 4" apart on ungreased cookie sheet. Bake at 325°F approximately 5 minutes.

Mrs. Lyndon B. Johnson (Lady Bird)

Former First Lady of the United States of America and Founder of National Wildflower Research Center. Austin, Texas, U.S.A.

WOMEN *to* WOMEN
A Gift of Hope

Company's Favourite Oat Squares

"This is my favourite Oat Squares recipe because no one makes oat squares like Cape Bretoners! This is my Mom's recipe. They are a big favourite with company."

1/2 cup Imperial margarine

1/2 cup white sugar

3 tsp boiling water

1 1/2 cup white flour

1/2 cup Crisco shortening

pinch of salt

1/2 tsp baking soda

1 1/2 cups rolled Quaker Oats

Mix the margarine, shortening, sugar, salt together and beat well with mixer. Add the baking soda to the boiling water and mix quickly, then add to the margarine mixture. Beat this well. Add flour and rolled oats and mix well. Sprinkle a small amount of flour on your counter and take half of your prepared recipe and roll it out with the rolling pin. Make it the thickness you desire. Cut into squares with a large knife. Repeat with the other half of the recipe mixture.

Put into an ungreased pan and bake in a 375°F oven for about seven minutes or until golden brown. Remove from pan and let cool on a cookie rack. These are very delicate when warm.

Bob Martin

Natalie MacMaster

Fiddler/Stepdancer
Port Hastings, Nova Scotia, Canada

"*I am honoured to be included in such a worthy project.*"

WOMEN to WOMEN
A Gift of Hope

Mom's Butter Tarts

"Whenever we think of Mom, (my sister, two brothers and I), we remember her humour, her warmth and her delicious buttertarts. She used to make them just to keep us away from the pies."

Pastry

1 1/2 cups flour	1/4 tsp salt
3/4 cup cold shortening, cubed	1/4 cup cold water

Filling

1/4 cup raisins or chopped walnuts, or both	1/2 cup corn syrup
	1 egg
1/4 cup softened butter	1 tsp white vinegar
1/2 cup brown sugar	1 tsp vanilla
	1/4 tsp salt

For pastry, in large bowl, stir together flour and salt. Cut in shortening with pastry blender until you get course crumbs. Using fork, stir in just enough water to make dough hold together. Form ball, wrap well and refrigerate 30 minutes.

In medium bowl, cream together butter and sugar (or sometimes Mom did this in a pan over a warm burner), then remove. Beat in syrup, egg, vinegar, vanilla and salt just until blended. Set aside.

On lightly floured surface, roll out 1/8" thick pastry. Use about 4" round cutter for muffin pan. Fit into cups. Sprinkle raisins and nuts evenly in each one. Spoon filling over (2/3 full).

Bake in preheated 375°F oven for 15 minutes or until pastry is a light golden colour. Filling should be runny.

Cool and enjoy.

Sherida Personal Management Inc.

Faye Dance

Broadcaster, Television Host
Toronto, Ontario, Canada

"My grandmother died of breast cancer at 64. My mom died of breast cancer at 64. May wonderful projects like this book help find a cure. This recipe is in her memory."

51

Victoria Sponge Cake

"This family recipe is a delicious treat to have at tea time."

To make two layers

4 oz self-rising flour
   (or plain flour and
   2 tsp baking powder)
pinch of salt
4 oz butter or margarine

4 oz castor sugar
2 eggs
1 tsp vanilla essence
1 to 2 tbsp milk or
   water to mix

Preheat oven to 380°F. Grease two 6–7" sponge sandwich tins and line with squares of greaseproof paper.

Sift flour and salt onto a piece of paper and set aside. Measure butter or margarine and sugar into a warmed mixing basin and beat well until pale and fluffy, about 8 to 10 minutes. Gradually add the lightly mixed eggs and vanilla essence. Beat the mixture well; if the egg is added too quickly the mixture may curdle.

Using a spoon, fold in half the flour. Then fold the milk or water into the mixture to give a medium-soft consistency.

Divide mixture equally between prepared tins and spread evenly. Place in the center of a moderately hot oven (380°F) and bake for 20 to 25 minutes. Remove cakes from oven and cool for five minutes in tins before turning out onto a wire tray. When cool, fill with your favourite jam or pudding and sprinkle with icing sugar.

Hon. Hilary M. Weston

Lieutenant Governor
of Ontario
Toronto, Ontario, Canada

Wacky Cake

"Growing up, my mom made this cake a lot. My brother was allergic to eggs so this is the perfect gooey chocolate cake without eggs. Plus, it's incredibly easy!"

1 1/2 cups flour	1 tsp baking powder
1 cup white sugar	1 tsp vanilla
3 tbsp cocoa	1 tbsp vinegar
1/2 tsp salt	5 tbsp melted butter
1 tsp baking soda	1 cup water

In square 8" pan sift all dry ingredients together. Make three wells in dry mixture. Pour vanilla into one, vinegar into another and melted butter into the third. Add one cup water and mix with fork. Bake in 350°F oven for 25 minutes. I like to finish it off with cream cheese icing!

Jill Krop

News Anchor, BCTV
Vancouver, British Columbia,
Canada

"Thanks for including me and I wish you much success!"

WOMEN *to* WOMEN
A Gift of Hope

Pound Cake

"My mother prepared this cake for each of the 8 figure and freestyle tests... I consider this a good omen cake, besides being delicious."

Beat well

1 lb butter

1 lb powdered sugar

6 eggs

Add

1 tsp vanilla extract

1 tsp lemon extract

Sift

3 cups cake flour and add to the above mixture.

Bake at 350°F for 1 hour in a well greased and floured bundt pan.

Remove from pan and after cooling, sprinkle with powdered sugar.

Kristi Yamaguchi

Professional Figure Skater
U.S., World and
Olympic Champion
Fremont, California, U.S.A.

Biscuits for my Doggie!
(Ellie, the dalmation)

"I enjoy cooking for my dog more than I do for myself. I love her."

1 cup white rice powder

1/4 cup soy flour

1 egg

1 tbsp unsulfered molasses

1/3 cup milk

1/3 cup powdered milk

2 tbsp safflower oil

Preheat oven to 350°F. Mix dry ingredients together. Add molasses, egg, oil and milk. Roll out flat onto oiled cookie sheet and cut into bite-sized pieces. Bake 20 minutes. Let cool and store in a tightly sealed container.

From the SPCA, Boston, MA

WOMEN to WOMEN
A Gift of Hope

My dalmation, Ellie, has a tendancy toward urinary stone formation, so I had to find treats that did not contain meat or meat by-products (low purine ingredients)… this is a great vegetarian snack for dogs. You can vary the recipe by throwing in grated carrots, cheese, sunflower seeds, or even some ground garlic.

Healthy… happy… Doggies!

Janice Ungaro

Morning Show Host
& Comedian
Z95.3 FM Radio
Vancouver, British Columbia,
Canada

Taking joy in life is a woman's best cosmetic.

Rosalind Russell

Highlights

Savoury and spicy accompaniments

Joy MacPhail's Risotto

"This makes a great dish first time around, but it's almost better as 'leftovers', a real plus for us working moms!!"

2 tbsp unsalted butter

2 tbsp olive oil

1/3 cup whole almonds, raw

1/2 cup fennel, sliced

1 medium onion, sliced

1 cup arborio rice

1 – 14 oz can tomatoes

1/2 cup peas

1 cup vegetable or chicken stock

1 cup white wine (or additional stock)

grated rind of 1/2 lemon

1/2 to 1 cup grated Parmesan cheese

salt and pepper to taste

Heat the butter and oil and sauté the whole almonds until golden. Remove from the pan.

Sauté the fennel and onion until transparent, then add the rice and cook, stirring until the rice grains glisten with the butter (it will also start to smell nutty).

WOMEN to WOMEN
A Gift of Hope

Warm stock and wine in separate pan. Add the tomatoes, peas, and some of the warm liquid and simmer. Keep adding small amounts of liquid as it is absorbed by the rice. This process will take about 45 minutes, but taste the rice to see if it's cooked, as you go.

When the rice is cooked, add the lemon rind, salt, pepper and Parmesan cheese to taste.

Serve it as a main meal with steamed green beans or a green salad or as a side dish with steamed vegetables and grilled fish steak, rosemary chicken breast or Italian sausage. This dish can be frozen, but it is better fresh. Leftovers make a great lunch.

Joy MacPhail

*Minister of Finance
and Corporate Relations,
Government of
British Columbia*
Victoria, British Columbia, Canada

*"I'm delighted to be able to contribute
in a small way to our collective fight
against breast cancer. Healthiness
paves a major path to economic
equality – which is my highest priority.
Best wishes for continued success with
this special project."*

Vegetable Stir-Fry with Cashew Nuts and Chili

"You can use any combination of vegetables you like in this recipe from Thailand cookery. Just start with the ones that take the longest to cook."

3/4 cup + 1 1/2 tbsp vegetable oil

1/2 cup cashew nuts

1 medium-large yellow onion

1 cup broccoli florets

1 cup peeled and finely sliced carrots

1 cup sliced long beans or green beans

1 cup water

1 cup sliced zucchini

1/2 cup sliced bamboo shoots

6 ears canned or frozen corn*

1 cup bean sprouts (optional)

1 tbsp very finely shredded fresh ginger

1 to 2 tsp sambal ulek or other chili paste

1 tbsp light soy sauce

1/2 tsp superfine white sugar

1/2 tsp salt

1 1/2 tsp corn starch

WOMEN to WOMEN
A Gift of Hope

Heat the 3/4 cup of oil in a small saucepan over high heat. When hot, add cashews. Cook, stirring and shaking the pan almost continuously, until they are barely golden, about 2 minutes. Retrieve with a slotted spoon. Set to drain on paper towels.

Slice onion, cut through stem end, then separate into layers.

Heat the 1 1/2 tbsp oil in a wok or skillet over high heat. Add the onion, broccoli, carrot and beans. Stir-fry for 2 minutes. Add 1/2 cup of the water and cover the pan. Allow the vegetables to steam-cook, stirring them occasionally, until almost crisp-tender, about 2 1/2 minutes.

Remove the lid, and keeping the heat on high, add the zucchini, bamboo shoots and corn. Stir-fry for about 1 1/2 minute.

Finally add the bean sprouts, ginger, chili paste, soy sauce, sugar and salt. Stir together until well mixed.

Stir the cornstarch into the remaining 1/2 cup water and pour over the vegetables. Stir over high heat until sauce thickens, about 1 1/2 minutes.

Add the cashews, transfer to a serving dish and serve at once.

*If using fresh miniature corn, parboil in a lightly salted boiling water for 2 minutes, then drain before stir-frying.

Ingrid Jensen

Ingrid Jensen

Jazz Musician
New York, New York, U.S.A.
(from Nanaimo, British Columbia, Canada)

"This is dedicated to the memory of Mercedes Rossi, a pianist friend who died in 1995 of cancer at age 33. Mercedes composed the poignant piece 'Ninety-One' which is on my second album 'Here On Earth'."

Tomatoes, Boccacini and Basil

"For me, as an Australian, summer is the best time of the year. Summer entertaining, especially preparing meals for friends that can be served outside on my flower-filled terrace, is one of my favourite leisure-time activities. I derive great pleasure from the natural beauty and taste of summer fruits, salads, vegetables and herbs and using these for culinary 'creations' that I offer to my guests. This 'recipe' is not really such; rather it is a description of one of the summer entrées I serve most often. I grow my own tomatoes and herbs and use them in making this."

Take very ripe, very fresh tomatoes, cut them in 1/4" slices and lay these slices in overlapping rings on a platter (one that complements the colour of the tomatoes).

Take boccacini cheese which can be obtained from your Italian supermarket or cheese shop (if you are feeling extravagant buy the original Buffalo variety imported from Italy, or buy a good local boccacini), slice and put a small piece of the cheese on top of each slice of tomato.

"It is most difficult to have a sense of joy, celebration and hope when we are sick and frightened. Yet, we need these healing emotions even more when we are in such a situation. In sharing food with friends, we can find the warmth, caring and even sometimes the laughter that we need. It would be wonderful if the recipes in this book could function as an off-beat 'medical prescription' for meals that would create this nurturing reality."

WOMEN to WOMEN
A Gift of Hope

64

Take fresh basil leaves (be very generous with the basil), roughly chop this and sprinkle over the tomatoes and cheese.

Just before serving, spoon over generous quantities of well-mixed vinaigrette dressing. It should be made according to the following recipe:

Vinaigrette dressing

1/4 tsp salt

1/3 tsp ground black pepper

1 tsp French Dijon mustard

1/2 tsp sugar

1 to 1 1/2 tbsp of good Italian balsamic vinegar (according to taste)

1/2 cup of good olive oil

Mix the salt, pepper, mustard and sugar with the balsamic vinegar, then slowly add the olive oil while beating the dressing with a fork. The quality of this dressing depends on the quality of the olive oil and balsamic vinegar used, use the best you can obtain. I vary the proportion of oil and vinegar both with the taste of the particular variety of oil or vinegar, and with characteristics of the other ingredients. For instance, with very sweet tomatoes, I would use slightly more vinegar, or indeed, if it were a very hot day and I wanted a stronger taste to the dressing.

Margaret A. Somerville (Margo)

University Professor, Gale Professor of Law; Professor, Faculty of Medicine; Founding Director, McGill Centre for Medicine Ethics and Law at McGill University Montreal, Quebec, Canada

Nadia's Eggplant Spread (Romanian "Salata de Vinete")

"This is an eggplant spread ideal on crackers, rye-krisps, or cocktail bread squares. It is a traditional Romanian recipe. My husband, Bart Conner's favourite."

2 medium sized eggplants (use very ripe eggplants)

2/3 cup of vegetable oil

1 medium white onion

4 tbsp "light" mayonnaise (we don't recommend fat-free)

1 tsp of Dijon mustard

pinch of salt

Pre-heat oven to 400°F. Place the eggplants on a non-stick cooking sheet in the oven and bake for about 80 minutes, rotating the eggplants every 20 minutes or so (be sure they are baked on all sides). Eggplants should be mushy when they are finished baking.

WOMEN to WOMEN
A Gift of Hope

Carefully put the eggplants in a zip-lock bag for ten minutes. Remove them from the bag, peel off the skin and throw the skin away. Put the eggplant "meat" into a strainer and drain it for about ten minutes.

On a cutting board, chop the eggplant until it becomes mashed like potatoes, and put it in a bowl.

With a wooden spoon, stir while slowly adding the oil. At this point the mixture will look pretty firm. Add the light mayonnaise and mustard. Stir until the mixture is complete.

Chop the onion into small 1/4" chunks and stir them into the mixture. Add salt to taste.

Refrigerate the mixture for about two hours.

Serve chilled with crackers, or breads of your choice.

Note: the true traditional Romanian style "Salata de Vinete" is served with roasted red peppers on the side. Enjoy!

Nadia's Eggplant Spread (Romanian "Salata de Vinete") is pictured on page 100.

Nadia Comaneci

Olympic Champion Gymnast from Romania
Norman, Oklahoma, U.S.A.

Tim Leyes

Erica Ehm

*TV Host, Actor, Songwriter and
Music Publisher*
Toronto, Ontario, Canada

Nona Moriani's Marinara Pasta Sauce

"Five years ago, my then boyfriend and I went to Italy. I was accompanying Steven on his pilgrimage to learn from his 98-year-old grandmother how to make the perfect basic pasta sauce. This is her recipe that I've adopted and adapted."

4 tbsp olive oil

1/2 cup chopped onion

a small can "Aurora" diced tomatoes

5 to 10 fresh basil leaves

1 garlic clove, chopped

2 tbsp cream or milk

1/2 tsp of salt and pepper

1/2 cup frozen peas

red pepper flakes for some zip, optional

parmesan cheese

Cook onions in olive oil on medium heat until edges start to turn brown. Add chopped tomatoes and bring to a boil. Add chopped garlic and basil. Simmer for 15 minutes. Add cream and blend half of sauce with hand blender. Salt and pepper to taste.

My twist to this perfect classic pasta sauce is to add some cut up veggies like broccoli and carrots for the last 4 minutes while you're boiling the pasta. Frozen peas add a nice touch.

Once pasta is ready, drain and put back into original pot. Add sauce, stir and then add grated Parmesan cheese to taste. "I like a lot."

WOMEN *to* WOMEN
A Gift of Hope

Oprah's Potatoes

2 1/2 lbs red potatoes

2 1/2 lbs Idaho potatoes

4 tbsp creamy pureed horseradish

1/2 cup Butter Buds Powder

2 cups skim milk

1 cup chicken stock

1/8 tsp Cayenne powder (optional)

1 1/2 tbsp ground black pepper

Wash potatoes well; leave the skin on; cut potatoes in half.

Place potatoes in kettle and fill with water to cover. Bring to a boil; reduce heat to low. Cover and simmer until potatoes are very tender.

Drain all water; add butter buds and begin to mash. Add chicken stock, skim milk, cayenne powder, horseradish, black pepper and mash until creamy but slightly lumpy.

Serves 12.

Oprah Winfrey

TV Talk Show Host, Actress
Chicago, Illinois, U.S.A.

Tomato and Mushroom Sauce (or Side Dish)

"This recipe can be used as a side dish or as a pasta sauce. It was a recipe that my sister Lisa found somewhere when she was newly married and was experimenting with gourmet cooking. I was a teenager and thought it was quite an exotic dish at the time. It's actually very nice to make in the winter when the veggies tend not to be as lush as they are in the summer. It tastes good even when those pale red cardboard tomatoes are all you can buy. It can all be made in one large frying pan."

5 slices bacon

2 tbsp very good olive oil

3 tomatoes seeded and liquid squeezed out

1 lb mushrooms (any kind), sliced

2 cloves of garlic, crushed

1 large onion, chopped

1 tsp oregano or Italian seasoning

lots of black pepper

WOMEN to WOMEN
A Gift of Hope

Dice and fry bacon (don't make it crispy). If you're worried about fat levels, drain off most of the bacon fat and add olive oil. Sauté onion and garlic until the onion becomes transparent. Add 1 lb of sliced mushrooms on medium heat until cooked (stop before there is a lot of liquid). Add oregano or Italian seasoning and diced and seeded tomatoes. Sauté on high until tomatoes are heated through. Add lots of black pepper and serve.

If sauce gets too wet and looks like soup instead of a side dish, you can throw in some low fat sour cream to rescue it before it goes to the table.

Jane Hawtin

*TV Talk Show Host of
"Jane Hawtin Live"*
Toronto, Ontario, Canada

*"Thanks for including me in
your book!"*

Deborra Hope

Journalist, Anchor –
"BCTV Noon News Hour"
Vancouver, British Columbia,
Canada

"I lost my beloved big sister,
Barbara, to cancer. I miss her every
day and I'm thrilled to share this
old family recipe in her honour.
All my best to you in this endeavour –
with apologies to 'The Spice Girls' –
there's nothing quite like
'Woman Power'!"

Deb's Family's Christmas Cheesies

"The source of almost all my recipes, my Mom. It's different. It's delicious. And it always conjures up warm, tasty memories of family Christmases past! These cheesies are really good all year round for a party snack. They look like cookies, but they're not sweet. A sort of cheesy shortbread, with a bit of crunch! I guarantee you'll love'em! (With due credit to my mom Isabel and my Aunt Hilda.)"

1 cup of butter (accept no substitutes)

8 oz (250g package) of McLaren's Imperial Cheddar Cheese (accept no substitutes)

2 cups flour

2 cups Rice Krispies

dash of Tobasco

dash of Worcestershire sauce

(and a tiny bit of cayenne if you like a bit more of a kick)

Preheat oven to 350°F.

Cream butter and the cheese. Add the rest of the ingredients. Knead or stir until you have a soft dough. You can spoon it out or roll it into cookie-sized balls. Flatten onto a ungreased cookie sheet (with a floured fork) and bake for 8 to 10 minutes.

Serve as an appetizer, or anytime as a snack.

WOMEN *to* WOMEN
A Gift of Hope

Granny's Tomato Juice

"Growing up in Toronto, we always went to my grandmother Petrie's for dinner every Sunday. As a 'teetotaller', she never served wine but made up for it with her special tomato juice which always started off every meal. I suppose you could add some vodka, but I've never tried as this version packs a fair punch all on its own."

1 quart (or litre) can
    of tomato juice

2 slices onion

1 bay leaf

3 to 4 tsp sugar

some salt

1/2 lemon squeezed

2 celery stalks and leaf
    (or more leaf and
    no stalk)

Let everything soak for at least 1/2 hour. Strain and enjoy. Chill if you wish.

Granny's Tomato Juice is pictured on page 101.

Anne Petrie

Broadcaster, Writer
Calgary, Alberta, Canada

"I had never thought about breast cancer in my own family until my grandmother died a few years ago and I was told she had been diagnosed and treated back in the 1930's. She lived well into her 9th decade. With better detection and therapies, I only hope that more women will have her good fortune."

Imagination is the highest kite one can fly.

Lauren Becall

Twilight

Light supper dishes for twilit evenings

Penne con Broccoli

"We discovered this dish on a trip to Spain. We couldn't get enough of this wonderful dish and we ordered it at almost every meal. Re-created in my kitchen."

1/8 cup olive oil (or more if needed)

1/2 stick butter

6 to 8 cloves fresh garlic, peeled and sliced

1 1/2 cups fresh mushrooms, sliced

1 1/2 to 2 cups grated Parmesan cheese

3/4 to 1 cup canned tomato sauce

2 fresh Roma tomatoes, chopped

1/2 cup raisins

1/2 cup pine nuts

2 cups steamed broccoli (cooked al dente)

Penne pasta, 1 – 16 oz box – De Cecco Brand (cooked al dente)

salt and pepper to taste

Prepare all ingredients as above. In a large frying pan, sauté the cloves of garlic in the olive oil. Add butter. When melted, slowly add Parmesan cheese, stirring constantly to get a thick soupy consistency. Add tomato sauce, still keeping that thickness. Keep heat low to medium.

Women to Women
A Gift of Hope

Add mushrooms. Add fresh tomatoes and cook al dente. You can add more cheese and tomato sauce to thicken or thin the sauce to your taste.

Add broccoli (they should be crunchy as they continue to cook in the sauce). Add raisins and pine nuts last, and simmer slowly for about 5 minutes.

Pour sauce over cooked Penne.

Penne con Broccoli is pictured on page 102.

Connie Sellecca

Actress
California, U.S.A.

"I am honoured to be involved in this worthy project. Wishing you great success, and kudos to everyone involved in Celebrity Lights II. *"*

Puttanesca
(Pasta of the Night)

"The thing with this recipe is that it is a dead steal from Diane Clement, but I make it so often now that all the people in my family think that I made it up, and I am not going to be the one to tell them otherwise... would you? Take the glory where you can.

"Over the years, Diane has provided scores of recipes for the happy listener, but the one I prepare the most is Puttanesca. This is a bone-simple pasta recipe that tastes so good you won't believe you made it yourself. It's a quickie, too, which is the reason it was developed in the first place. Ladies of the night in Stena found it a boon to time management."

You must not leave out the anchovies – they are an essential element. The fish taste disappears in the cooking and even anchovy haters won't be able to tell. One other thing about anchovies – use them immediately after opening the tin. Don't let them sit around for too long as they get funky, which is why so many people hate them.

If you are in a huge hurry, you can simply chop up all the tomato mixture ingredients, throw them into a large heavy skillet, simmer for 10 to 15 minutes, and carry on with the rest of the recipe.

8 to 10 medium
tomatoes, in
1/2" slices

2 small cans anchovies,
drained, patted dry
and chopped

1/2 cup black pitted
olives, chopped

5 cloves garlic,
finely chopped

1/2 tsp dried crushed red
pepper flakes

1 cup fresh basil

olive oil

1 to 1 1/2 lbs
dried spaghetti
(or penne or fettaccine)

1 cup freshly grated
Parmigiano-Reggiano
(or asiago)

freshly ground pepper

Preheat oven to 350°F. In a large lasagne-type
pan about 12 x 15", make two layers each of
the tomatoes, anchovies, olives, garlic, pepper
flakes and 1/2 cup of the basil, in that order.
Drizzle each layer well with olive oil and
a good sprinkling of black pepper. Bake for
30 to 35 minutes.

In the meantime, cook the pasta. Drain and
put in large serving bowls and toss with a little
bit of olive oil and half of the cheese. Chop up
the baked tomato mixture and add to the
pasta. Add the rest of the cheese and the rest
of the basil.

Serve with crusty Italian bread to mop up the
juice, and offer more grated cheese and black
pepper to taste.

Serves 6.

Vicki Gabereau

*Host of Vancouver Television's
"Gabereau Live"*
Vancouver, British Columbia,
Canada

Linguine al Limone

"This recipe was passed on to me by a good friend and I only make it during happy times. Therefore, it makes the times I make it, happy."

Margot Franssen

President and Partner of
"The Body Shop Canada"
Don Mills, Ontario, Canada

"The secret of life is to live it."

2 lemons

1 lb linguine or spaghetti, preferably fresh

1 cup whipping cream

1/4 cup brandy

3/4 cup Parmesan cheese, freshly grated

2 tbsp butter

freshly ground pepper to taste

Carefully remove a thin layer of rind from lemons using a vegetable peeler. Mince very finely. There will be about 2 tbsp. Set aside. Remove all of the white pith from lemons and section flesh, discarding membranes and seeds. Set aside. Cook linguine in lots of boiling salted water until al dente. Meanwhile, in a small heavy saucepan over low heat, bring cream, brandy and lemon pulp to a boil. Boil gently for 7 to 8 minutes until slightly reduced. Place drained linguine in a large, warm bowl and toss with butter. Add sauce and toss to combine. Add cheese and toss again. Serve immediately with reserved lemon zest.

Serves 6.

WOMEN *to* WOMEN
A Gift of Hope

Pasta Brie & Fresh Tomatoes

"I have been a vegetarian for 15 years and this is quick as I am always in a hurry. It's nutritious, colourful and absolutely delicious."

4 ripe large tomatoes cut into cubes

1 lb brie cheese, cut into pieces (rind off)

1 cup cleaned, fresh basil leaves cut into strips

3 garlic cloves, minced

1 cup and 1 tbsp olive oil

2 1/2 tsp pepper

1 1/2 lbs linguini or tagliatelle

Fresh grated parmesan cheese

Combine everything (except pasta, tbsp oil and Parmesan cheese) at least 2 1/2 hours ahead of time (can even be combined in morning). At mealtime, cook pasta in water with 1 tbsp oil.

Drain pasta when done. Mix well with the tomato/brie elixir (Brie should melt).

Sprinkle with fresh parmesan.

To be accompanied with crusty French bread, green salad and avocados.

Hayley Mills

Actress
London, England

WOMEN *to* WOMEN
A Gift of Hope

81

Gin-Gingered Prawns

"One of my all-time hits, this appetizer or first
course prawn dish hails from 'down under'.
Prepare it at the last minute in front of your
guests so the aroma of the ginger, gin and onion
will titillate their taste buds. You can have
everything ready to go before your guests arrive,
then cook up a storm. Pickled Japanese ginger
can be found at most specialty Oriental markets
(or beg some from a Japanese restaurant.)
Allow 5 to 6 prawns per person; about
30 medium sized prawns will serve 6.

4 to 5 tbsp
   unsalted butter

2/3 cup finely chopped
   green onion

30 medium sized raw
   prawns, peeled

1 to 2 tbsp pickled
   Japanese ginger,
   well drained

3 tbsp gin

1 loaf baguette bread,
   thinly sliced
   and warmed

WOMEN to WOMEN
A Gift of Hope

Just before serving: Melt butter in large frypan. Add onions and sauté briefly. Add prawns and sauté only until lightly opaque. Add ginger and gin and continue to cook for a minute or two longer, just until prawns are opaque. Do not overcook. Serve with toothpicks or in scallop shells. Pass warm bread for dipping into the sauce.

Note: For more people, if you increase the number of prawns, you must also increase the amount of sauce. There must be plenty for dipping.

Gin-Gingered Prawns are pictured on page 103.

Diane Clement

Cookbook Author,
Canadian Best-selling
Chef on the Run *Series;*
Chef/Owner,
"Tomato Fresh Food Cafe"
Vancouver, British Columbia,
Canada

"To share in the 'Gift of Hope Celebrity Lights' with my passion for writing about food is indeed an honour. Celebrity Lights II will be another winner. Thanks for including me!"

Crab Cakes

"From the Chef of President and Mrs. Gerald R. Ford, Chef Lorraine M. Ornelas. This recipe is one that the Ford family has always enjoyed."

1 lb crab meat
  (fresh or frozen)

1 stalk celery,
  finely chopped

2 green onions,
  finely chopped

1 tbsp fresh cilantro,
  finely chopped

1 tsp fresh basil,
  finely chopped

2 egg whites

1 tbsp low-fat
  mayonnaise

1 tbsp bread crumbs

1 cup bread crumbs

12 lemon wedges

olive oil (spray)

mixed baby greens

Heat oven to 400°F. Mix crab, celery, onions, cilantro, basil, egg whites, mayonnaise and 1 tbsp bread crumbs. If using fresh crab, do not over mix, chunks could be kept intact.

WOMEN to WOMEN
A Gift of Hope

Using mixture, mold six, equal-sized cakes at approximately 1/4 cup each. Cover cakes with bread crumbs and set aside. Cakes will be very delicate.

Place three cakes in medium-heated, 12" sauté pan, and coat heavily with olive oil spray. Turn cakes after approximately two minutes , or when golden brown. Remove cakes after approximately two more minutes and place on cookie sheet. Repeat with remaining three cakes.

Place cakes and cookie sheet in 400°F oven for 15 minutes, or until thoroughly cooked. Remove from oven, and serve immediately on plate garnished with mixed greens and lemon wedges.

Crab Cakes are pictured on page 104.

Betty Ford

*Former First Lady of
the United States of America,
and Co-founder of the
Betty Ford Center
Rancho Mirage, California, U.S.A.*

Annette Funicello

Singer/Actress
Encino, California, U.S.A.

Chicken Bailey

"My daughter, Gina and I cook this together. It is quick, easy, non-fattening, delicious!"

*4 boneless, skinless
  chicken breasts
2 tbsp cooking oil
low-sodium soy sauce*

*hot English mustard
2 garlic cloves, chopped
1 tsp salt
1 tsp pepper*

Add cooking oil to fry pan. Cube chicken and place into pan. Paint mustard evenly over chicken. Add garlic to chicken. Cover chicken with soy sauce. Add salt and pepper.

Stir-fry all ingredients together until chicken is completely cooked and mixture has absorbed into chicken.

Serve on top of steamed rice with broccoli.

Enjoy… we do… it's delicious.

Serves 4.

Chicken Bailey is pictured on page 105.

WOMEN *to* WOMEN
A Gift of Hope

Shirley's "Partridge" Skewers

1 lb cubed beef	egg for dipping
1 lb cubed pork	cracker crumbs
1 lb cubed veal	butter or margarine
8 or 10 wooden skewers	herbs to taste

On each skewer, alternate a piece of beef, pork and veal all the way down the line. Dip entire skewers into egg and cracker crumbs until completely covered. Brown on top of stove in butter or margarine until it's brown on all sides. Place in covered casserole, salt and pepper, herbs of your taste and dot with butter.

Bake at 300°F for about 1 hour and 45 minutes. Baste a few times, uncover and bake 1/2 hour more. Serve with rice or buttered noodles.

Shirley Jones

Actress/Singer
Los Angeles, California, U.S.A.

Shirley's "Partridge" Skewers are pictured on page 106.

WOMEN to WOMEN
A Gift of Hope

Easy Chicken Rollups

4 boneless, skinless chicken breasts	several toothpicks
1 small tin tomato paste	1 tin chicken broth
2 tbsp olive oil	1 tbsp balsamic vinegar
4 ounces feta cheese	2 tbsp cornstarch

Put each chicken breast between pieces of wax paper and gently pound flat with a meat mallet. Spread about one tablespoon of tomato paste on each one, and crumble about an ounce of feta cheese onto the spread tomato paste.

Beginning at the narrow end of the chicken breast, gently roll it up and secure with one or two toothpicks.

Place on baking sheet and brush lightly with olive oil. Bake at 325°F for one hour.

Fifteen minutes before serving, put chicken broth into a small saucepan. Add cornstarch that has been mixed with a small amount of water. Blend the cornstarch well with the broth, and then add the balsamic vinegar. Bring slowly to a boil, stirring constantly until it thickens.

Once chicken is removed from oven, take out the toothpicks, place on the serving plate, and pour a small pool of the chicken broth sauce around it. Enjoy!

Lee Mackenzie

*Host of
"CHEK News at Noon"
Victoria, British Columbia, Canada*

WOMEN *to* WOMEN
A Gift of Hope

Kottbullar
(Swedish Meatballs)

"My favourite family recipe because of childhood memories of wonderful food and family gatherings."

1 lb ground round,
* finely ground*

1/2 cup dry
* bread crumbs*

1 egg, slightly beaten

1/3 tsp salt

1/4 tsp pepper

few grains nutmeg

2 to 3 slices salt pork
* or bacon*

1 bouillon cube

Mix and make into small balls using as little pressure as possible. Brown in hot fat from salt pork or bacon. Remove. Add 2 tbsp butter and stir in 2 tbsp flour until well blended. Add 2 cups water with a bouillon cube dissolved in it. Bring to boil, then add meatballs. Let simmer 1 1/2 hours covered. For best flavour, reheat next day.

Double or triple as needed.

Barbara Barde

Television Executive Producer
Toronto, Ontario, Canada

"This is dedicated to the memory of Loretta Erikson, my cousin who died of breast cancer."

Barbara Walters' Mother's Stuffed Cabbage Rolls

3 lbs lean ground chuck

regular salt to taste

3/4 tsp pepper

2 tsp celery salt
  or to taste

1/2 cup ketchup

2 eggs

1/2 cup crushed,
  unsalted crackers

2 heads (2 lbs each)
  green cabbage

6 quarts boiling water

3 cups chopped onion

2 bottles (12 oz each or
  2 cups) chili sauce

1 jar (12 oz or 1 cup)
  grape jelly

1/4 cup water

In large bowl, combine meat, regular salt, pepper, celery salt, ketchup, eggs and crackers. Mix with hands just until mixture is well combined. Cut out and discard hard centre core of cabbage.

Place cabbage in large kettle. Pour 6 quarts boiling water over it. Let stand until leaves are flexible and can be easily removed from head, about 5 minutes. If necessary, return cabbage to hot water to soften inner leaves.

WOMEN *to* WOMEN
A Gift of Hope

Using a 1/4 cup measure, scoop up a scant 1/4 cup of the meat mixture. With hands, form into rolls, 3 inches long and 1 inch wide, making about 28 rolls in all. Place each meat roll on a drained cabbage leaf. Fold top of leaf over meat, then fold in sides and roll up into an oblong shape. Continue rolling remaining meat rolls and cabbage leaves.

In bottom of lightly greased 11 1/2 x 12 x 2 1/4-inch roasting pan, spread chopped onion evenly. Arrange cabbage rolls in neat rows on top of onion. In a 2-quart saucepan, combine chili sauce, grape jelly and 1/4 cup water. Heat over medium heat, stirring, until jelly melts. Pour over cabbage rolls. Cover pan tightly with foil.

Bake in preheated 375°F oven 2 hours. Remove foil. Brush rolls with sauce. Continue to bake, uncovered, 40 minutes or until sauce is thick and syrupy and cabbage rolls are glazed. Serve rolls with sauce spooned over them.

Makes 28 cabbage rolls to serve 14.

Barbara Walters

Telvision Broadcast Journalist, Host of ABC's "20/20"
New York, New York, U.S.A.

New Salsa Cheeseburgers

"These robust burgers are easy to throw together from ingredients in my fridge, and everyone loves them. Chopped cilantro makes a nice addition."

Whisk together

1 egg	1/2 tsp salt
1/4 cup salsa	1/4 tsp cayenne pepper
1/2 tsp cumin	1/4 tsp black pepper

Stir in

1/4 cup fine dry bread crumbs

Add

1 lb ground beef and blend,
    using a fork or your hands

Work in

1/2 cup grated cheddar, Fontina or Asiago cheese

WOMEN to WOMEN
A Gift of Hope

Work with a fork or your hands until just blended. Over mixing toughens meat. Shape into 4 patties, each about 3/4" thick. Place patties on an oiled, preheated grill and barbecue, covered, for 6 to 8 minutes per side for well-done burgers.

Makes 4 burgers.

Jazz up ground beef with spicy salsa and whatever cheese you have on hand. Serve on fresh Kaiser rolls topped with fiery salsa, nippy cheddar or guacamole.

A New Salsa Cheeseburger is pictured on page 107.

Rona Maynard

Editor, Chatelaine Magazine
Toronto, Ontario, Canada

The way I see it, if you want the rainbow,
you gotta put up with the rain.

Dolly Parton

Candlelight

Full entrées and hearty dishes for dinner

WOMEN to WOMEN

A Gift of Hope

Grilled Fish with Papaya Salsa

"This is one of my favourite menu items in the summer when everything is fresh and readily available. Simple and elegant!"

Salsa

1 cup red bell peppers, seeded and diced into 1/2" cubes

1/2 cup yellow peppers, seeded and diced into 1/2" cubes

1 jalapeno pepper, seeded and finely chopped

1 1/2 to 2 cups papaya, peeled and diced into 1" cubes

1 clove roasted garlic, mashed

1 cup red onion, finely chopped

1/2 cup fresh cilantro

1/2 cup fresh basil

2 limes, juiced

Prepare peppers, papaya and onion as above. Julienne cilantro and basil into very thin strips. Combine all salsa ingredients and let stand at least 2 hours.

Fish

4 white fish steaks,   salt and pepper
   1 to 1 1/2" thick
   (halibut or tuna)

Salt and pepper fish steaks to taste. Grill fish steaks on barbecue to desired doneness (tuna – medium rare; halibut – medium).

Spoon papaya salsa onto plates and top with grilled fish steaks. Serve accompanied by: rice with herbs, tart green salad, fresh spinach sautéed with garlic, and crusty rolls.

Barbara Amster

Senior Vice-President, Marketing & Sales, Canadian Airlines International Ltd.
Calgary, Alberta, Canada

"It is always a pleasure to assist such a worthy cause."

Always be a first-rate version of yourself,
instead of a second-rate version of somebody else.

Judy Garland

Rita's Tea Room Cinnamon Buns,
from Rita MacNeil. See page 25.

Nadia's Eggplant Spread (Romanian "Salata de Vinete"), from Nadia Comaneci. See page 66.
Tabbouli Salad, from Marlo Thomas. See page 43.

Granny's Tomato Juice,
from Anne Petrie. See page 73.

**Penne con Broccoli,
from Connie Sellecca. See page 76.**

Gin-Gingered Prawns,
from Diane Clement. See page 82.

**Crab Cakes,
from Betty Ford. See page 84.**

Chicken Bailey,
from Annette Funicello. See page 86.

Shirley's 'Partridge' Skewers,
from Shirley Jones. See page 87.

New Salsa Cheeseburgers,
from Rona Maynard. See page 92.

**Hungarian Chicken à la Schlemmertopf,
from Katarina Witt. See page 111.**

Crunchy Pie,
from Betty White. See page 143.

**Fresh Strawberry Tarte,
from Carole Taylor. See page 144.**

Hungarian Chicken à la Schlemmertopf

"One of my favourite recipes. This meal is very easy to prepare in a German clay-baker (f.e. Schlemmertopf)."

*1 frying chicken
  (3 1/2 to 4 lbs),
  cut in serving pieces*

2 large onions, chopped

1 green pepper, chopped

*1 1/2 tbsp Hungarian
  paprika*

salt and pepper

*4 medium potatoes, cut
  as for French frying*

*1 cup sour cream
  (optional)*

4 pieces of bacon, sliced

Put bacon, onions and green pepper into the Schlemmertopf. Add the salted and peppered chicken pieces, sprinkle with paprika. Cover and bake at 425°F for 20 minutes. Add potatoes and bake for another 60 minutes. Remove Schlemmertopf from oven, add sour cream, cover and let stand for 5 minutes.

Serve with crusty French bread.

*Hungarian Chicken à la Schlemmertopf
is pictured on page 108.*

Katarina Witt

*Olympic Champion and
Professional Figure Skater*
Germany

*"Wishing you a lot of success
with the project."*

Spiced Salmon

"I love salmon and all that is
sweet and sour, exotic…"

3/4 cup plus
   2 tbsp honey

1 tsp ground cumin

1 tsp curry powder

1 tsp paprika

1 tsp black pepper

2 tbsp soy sauce

1 tbsp nuoc mam,
   Oriental fish sauce

4 salmon steaks
   (1/2 lb each)

1 cup quick-cooking
   couscous

1 carrot, finely diced

1 small zucchini,
   finely diced

1/2 red pepper,
   finely diced

2 tbsp olive oil

2 cups sunflower oil

2 leeks, finely julienned

In a heavy medium-sized saucepan, mix together
the honey, cumin, curry powder, paprika, black
pepper, soy and fish sauces. Cook over a very
low flame for 30 minutes. Meanwhile, heat
a non-stick pan over a medium-high flame.

WOMEN to WOMEN
A Gift of Hope

Place the salmon steaks, skin side down, in the hot pan and cook until the skin is crisp. Turn the salmon. Cook until the fish flakes easily. Remove to a platter and baste with the spiced honey. Keep hot.

While the salmon is cooking, prepare the couscous. In a medium saucepan with a cover, bring 1 1/2 cups of salted water to a boil. Add the couscous and carrot, zucchini, and red pepper. Stir until all of the water is absorbed. Remove the pot from the heat, cover, and let rest 5 minutes. Fluff the couscous with a fork. Add the olive oil and continue to rake with the fork until no lumps remain. Cover and keep hot.

Heat the sunflower oil in a deep skillet. Fry the leeks in the oil until crisp. Drain on paper towels.

To serve: Pack 1/4 of the couscous into a shallow bowl. Turn the packed couscous out onto a serving platter, flatten with a spatula, and top with a salmon steak. Repeat with the remaining portions. Pour some of the hot honey around the couscous. Sprinkle the leeks over the fish.

Serves 4.

Francine Pelletier

Writer/Broadcaster for CBC's Current Affairs Program "The Fifth Estate"
Toronto, Ontario, Canada

"A women's cookbook is way overdue. Bravo!"

Coulibiac of Fresh Lobster and Salmon

"It's sooo good! Plus, when I'm penny pinching, I substitute canned tuna for the lobster (which I always buy canned and frozen too) and it's still spectacular. You can also use milk to reduce (or eliminate) the fat content of the cream.

"The plump brioche conceals layers of pink decadence… lobster cloaked in a cheesy wine sauce and salmon dressed with rice. An extravagant dish perfect for a gathering of very special friends."

Cheese Sauce

6 tbsp butter

6 tbsp flour

3 cups table cream (18%)

1 cup grated Gruyere cheese (about 1/4 lb)

3/4 cup white wine

1 tsp ground or freshly grated nutmeg

salt and pepper to taste

Rice mixture

3/4 cup parboiled rice cooked in 1 cup water (Uncle Ben's Converted is ideal for this dish)

3 eggs, hard-boiled and diced 1/4" thick

1/3 cup finely chopped green onions

WOMEN to WOMEN
A Gift of Hope

Filling

9 lobsters (1 1/2 lbs
  each), cooked, shelled
  and diced 1/2"

4 tbsp fresh tarragon or
  1 tbsp dried tarragon

4 tbsp chopped fresh
  dill weed or 1 tbsp
  dried dill

4 tbsp chopped fresh
  parsley or 1 tbsp
  dried parsley

3 lbs salmon fillets,
  sliced diagonally,
  1/8", as one would
  slice smoked salmon

salt and pepper to taste

Brioche

1 1/2 pkg dry
  active yeast

3 tbsp warm water

3 tbsp sugar

3/4 tsp salt

3 tbsp butter,
  melted and cooled

9 tbsp milk

3 eggs, lightly beaten

2 1/2 cups flour

Shirley McQueen

Actor/Broadcaster
Vancouver, British Columbia,
Canada

*"Breast cancer has had an impact
on our family. My mother Loraine
McCormick is a survivor, having
undergone a single mastectomy
tram-flap in 1996. Her older sister,
my Aunty Vivian, succumbed to
the disease in 1976."*

To make cheese sauce, melt butter in a small heavy saucepan over medium heat. Whisk in flour and brown lightly. Slowly add cream, whisking continuously. Still whisking, bring mixture to a light boil. It will be thick at that point. Turn off heat. Stir in cheese until melted. Add wine, nutmeg, salt and pepper. Whisk until smooth and well blended. Set aside.

In a mixing bowl combine cooked rice, diced eggs, green onions and 3/4 cup of cheese sauce.

In another bowl mix diced lobster and herbs with remaining cheese sauce.

Lightly butter a large shallow baking dish. Spread the rice and egg mixture in an even layer on the bottom. Then, layer on half of the salmon

continued on next page

slices and season with a little salt and pepper.
On top of that, spread the lobster mixture.
Finish with the remaining salmon slices,
seasoned with a little salt and pepper.
(The dish can be refrigerated at this point, to
be finished as much as a day later. Remove
from the refrigerator 2 hours before baking.)

Preheat oven to 400°F.

For brioche, dissolve yeast in warm water
sprinkled with sugar. Mix in salt, butter, milk,
eggs and 1 1/2 cups of flour. Beat with electric
beater on low speed to blend ingredients.
Increase beater speed to medium and beat for
2 minutes. Add remaining flour. Beat until
smooth and let rise in a warm place for 1/2 to
1 hour, or until doubled in bulk. Stir down with
a spoon and pour over casserole, spreading
gently to cover filling. Let stand, uncovered,
for 10 minutes.

Bake for 30 to 45 minutes, or until top is golden
brown and filling is heated through. After
removing from the oven, brush the crust with
melted butter, if you wish. The coulibiac is a
great dish for a buffet, since it will retain its own
heat for a long time, and is good at room
temperature as well. Serve with Herb and
Lemon Sauce. Serves 15.

WOMEN to WOMEN
A Gift of Hope

Oriental Barbecued Salmon

A great blend of Eastern and Western flavours...

3 tbsp dry white wine

3 tbsp dark soy sauce

2 tbsp firmly packed
  brown sugar

1 tbsp soy sauce

1 tsp oriental sesame oil

1 1/2 lbs of 1" thick
  salmon steaks
  or 1 1/2 lbs
  filleted salmon

1 large bunch
  spinach leaves

1 medium papaya,
  peeled, seeded, sliced
  into 1/4" slices

Stir first 5 ingredients in small bowl until sugar dissolves. Place salmon in non-aluminum pan and pour marinade over. Cover and refrigerate for 3 hours, turning salmon occasionally. Prepare barbecue grill, adjusting rack 1 1/2" from fire. Line platter with spinach. Generously grease grill rack. Transfer salmon to grill rack, reserving marinade. Cook until salmon is just opaque, about 9 minutes per inch thickness, turning just once. Meanwhile simmer reserved marinade in heavy small saucepan until reduced to 4 tablespoons, stirring frequently (about 6 minutes). Transfer fish to spinach lined platter. Spoon marinade over and garnish with papaya. Serve immediately.

Serves 4.

Wendy Robson

Artist
Nanaimo British Columbia, Canada

"Sooner or later, everyone is touched by this disease. Cancer is everyone's concern... we must fight for a cure and support those who have survived the battle."

WOMEN *to* WOMEN
A Gift of Hope

Two Fish in Phyllo

"This recipe is from my brother Michel Rabu, chef and owner of the 'Gourmet by the Sea' restaurant in Campbell River, British Columbia. Having eaten foods from all over the world, while touring, I still find that my brother's creations are the healthiest and most delectable. I therefore promise not to cook and my brother promises not to sing! It's a good deal!"

4 pieces of fresh salmon
  filet (1 x 1 x 4")
4 pieces of fresh halibut
  (1 x 1 x 4")
4 sheets of phyllo pastry

8 leaves sorrel or
  spinach
4 tsp of Bernaise sauce
8 tbsp of melted butter

Lay phyllo sheet on flat surface, paint on melted butter with pastry brush, fold sheet in half.

Lengthwise at one end, stack 1 sorrel or spinach leaf, 1 piece of salmon and 1 piece of halibut.

Add a bit of Bernaise sauce and cover with second sorrel or spinach leaf.

WOMEN to WOMEN

A Gift of Hope

Fold each side of phyllo about 1" in toward the centre, roll phyllo to the end as you would a Chinese egg roll. Paint remaining butter on phyllo roll. Bake in 375°F oven for approximately 7 minutes or until golden. Turn over and bake other side until golden (approximately 7 minutes).

Prepare Guava Sauce (recipe below) while baking fish.

Serve on Basmati rice with stirfried snow peas, grilled red peppers. Top with guava sauce.

Guava Sauce

6 oz guava nectar

6 oz pineapple juice

1 tsp Madras curry

1 tbsp arrowroot mixed with 2 tbsp water

In a sauce pan bring nectar and juice to a boil. Mix in curry, add arrowroot mixture. Simmer and stir for 2 minutes. Keep sauce warm until ready to serve on fish.

Joëlle Rabu

Singer/Songwriter,
Stage Actor, Mother
Nanaimo, British Columbia, Canada

"May this Celebrity Lights II *cookbook be in celebration of the cure."*

Pan Roasted Seabass with a Mustard Sauce

"This is a light dish even with that little bit of cream and I love seabass. Presentation is great and it is so quick!!"

Mustard Sauce

1/2 cup fish stock
1/2 cup 35% cream

1/2 cup finely diced fennel
2 tbsp grainy mustard

Place the fish stock, cream and fennel in a pan and bring to a boil to reduce by half. Remove the pan from the heat and stir in the mustard. Season with salt and pepper. (If you choose to hold the sauce, add the mustard after you reheat, just prior to serving.)

Note: Mustard is acidic and will become bitter if it cools, so add it off the heat.

1 1/2 lbs seabass,
portioned, skin left on
and scored

salt and pepper

2 tbsp olive oil

Season the fish with salt and pepper. Heat the olive oil in a pan and sear the seabass skin side down for 1 1/2 minutes, then flip over and sear the other side for 30 seconds. Then place in the oven for 5 minutes.

Remove and let stand.

Drizzle the warm mustard sauce on the plate and place the seabass on top. Lay steamed asparagus to the side.

Serve immediately. Serves 4.

Beverly Topping

*Chairman and Chief Officer
of "Today's Parent Group"*
Toronto, Ontario, Canada

*"I am passionate about food and life!
I am a breast cancer survivor and
am committed to fundraising research.
Thank you for including me
in this project."*

Sea Bass in A Couscous Crust

"This recipe is from Bonnie Stern's *More Heart Smart Cooking*. It's fabulous, no fail and luxurious. After making it more than two dozen times, I asked Bonnie to be my bridesmaid! She said 'yes'."

The couscous adds a great texture, and the vinaigrette keeps the fish moist. Halibut and salmon are also delicious cooked this way. The vinaigrette is also delicious on salads.

3/4 cup couscous

3/4 cup boiling water
    or homemade
    chicken stock

1 tsp ground cumin

1/2 tsp salt

1/2 cup all-purpose
    flour

1 egg or 2 egg whites,
    beaten

6 sea bass fillets,
    1" thick, skin
    removed (4oz each)

1 tbsp olive oil

10 cups mixed
    salad greens

Tomato Olive Vinaigrette

2 tbsp red wine vinegar

2 tbsp lemon juice

1 clove garlic, minced

1/2 tsp pepper

1/4 cup tomato juice

2 tbsp olive oil

2 tbsp chopped
sun-dried tomatoes

2 tbsp shredded
fresh basil or
chopped parsley

salt to taste

Place couscous in shallow baking dish. Combine boiling water with cumin and salt and pour over couscous. Cover tightly with foil and allow to rest for 15 minutes. Fluff with fork and reserve.

Place flour in shallow dish. Place beaten egg in second shallow dish.

Pat fish dry. Dip fish into flour and shake off excess. Dip into egg and allow excess to drip off. Pat couscous into fish to coat all over. Refrigerate until ready to cook.

For vinaigrette, in bowl, combine vinegar, lemon juice, garlic and pepper. Whisk in tomato juice and oil. Stir in tomatoes, basil and salt.

Heat 1 tbsp olive oil in non-stick oven proof skillet on high heat. Add fish and cook for 1 minute. Turn gently and cook for 1 minute longer. Transfer to preheated 425°F oven and bake for 10 minutes or until cooked through.

Serve fish on salad greens and drizzle with vinaigrette.

Makes 6 servings.

Shelagh Rogers

*Broadcaster, Arts Journalist
and National Volunteer for
Frontier College, Canada's
largest literacy network.*
Toronto, Ontario, Canada

*"I look at my family, friends and
their families and see no life is
untouched by breast cancer.
This is such a joyous, positive project,
and there is such potential in it.
Cue the applause!"*

Renee's Indonesian Chicken

"This is easy to make, it's delicious and my three children love it. Besides, it reminds me of my mother's cooking, which is fabulous."

3 lbs chicken legs, skinned and separated into thighs and drumsticks

1 tbsp vegetable oil

2 tsp finely minced fresh ginger

3 cloves garlic, minced

1/2 cup Kecap manis (sweet soy sauce)*

2 slices fresh lemon, seeds removed

1 tbsp water

1 tsp corn starch

Heat oil in a large, non-stick skillet with a tight-fitting lid. Brown chicken pieces in hot oil for a few minutes on each side. Set chicken aside. Drain oil from pan. Add ginger and garlic and fry for about 1 minute. Add Kecap manis.

"My grandmother was of mixed European-Indonesian heritage. She married a Dutchman who had immigrated to Indonesia in the early part of this century and bore him six children. She contracted breast cancer in her late 30's and died of complications related to the disease when she was 40. Her youngest child, my mother, was six years old at the time. I never knew my grandmother but I think often of her and what must have been a terrible ordeal, given Indonesia had little in the way of medical services at the time. I've dedicated the recipe I'm submitting to her memory."

Place chicken in pan, spooning sauce over each piece. Tuck lemon pieces on each side of pan. Turn heat to low, cover tightly and let simmer for about 10 minutes. Uncover and turn chicken pieces. If chicken looks dry, add about a tbsp of water, cover again and let cook another 10 to 15 minutes or until cooked through.

When finished cooking, remove chicken pieces from pan and place in a serving bowl. Cover and keep warm while finishing the sauce. Remove lemon pieces from sauce. In a small bowl, combine water and corn starch and stir until smooth. Add several spoonfuls of sauce to corn starch mixture, stir until thoroughly combined and add slowly to sauce, stirring all the time.

Turn heat to high and bring sauce to a boil and cook until thickened, about two minutes. Pour over chicken and serve with plain steamed rice and Indonesian sambal on the side for those who like it spicy.

Serves 6.

*Kecap manis or Ketjap manis can be found in Asian stores or supermarkets that carry Asian foods. My favourite brand is ABC.

Ric Ernst

Renee Blackstone

Journalist/Living Editor
"The Province" Newspaper
Vancouver, British Columbia, Canada

Herbed Swordfish Steaks

"I'm not a brave barbecuer, and I have found this recipe to be foolproof, delicious and it wows the guests!"

1/4 cup minced
   fresh parsley

1/4 cup olive oil

2 tbsp lemon juice

2 cloves garlic, minced

1 tbsp chopped
   fresh oregano
   (or 1 tsp dried)

2 tsp Dijon mustard

1/2 chopped fresh thyme
   or 1/4 tsp dried thyme

1/2 tsp pepper

1 1/2 lbs swordfish
   or shark steak
   (3/4" thick)

salt

In shallow dish large enough to hold steaks in single layer, mix together parsley, oil, lemon juice, garlic, oregano, mustard, thyme and pepper. Add steaks, turning to coat well; cover and marinate for 30 minutes at room temperature or 1 hour in refrigerator, turning often.

Remove steaks, reserving any marinade. Cook on greased grill over hot coals or on high setting for 3 to 4 minutes or until steaks are well marked. Turning carefully and brushing lightly with marinade, cook for 3 to 4 minutes longer or until fish flakes easily when tested with fork. Season with salt to taste.

Serve these easy steaks with grilled tomato slices drizzled with olive oil. For a new twist, substitute shark for swordfish.

Makes 4 servings.

Tina Srebotnjak

Host, "Midday," CBC TV
Toronto, Ontario, Canada

Cowichan Bay Farms "Pastured" Chicken

Braised in Beer with Chantrelle Mushrooms, Leeks, Bacon and Sage

- 1 large pastured or free range chicken (3 to 5 lbs)
- 1 cup white of leek, sliced lengthwise and diced
- 1/4 cup good quality smoked bacon, diced
- 1 cup fresh chantrelle mushrooms, cut in half or quartered
- 2 tbsp fresh, chopped garlic
- 1 cup chicken stock
- 1 cup microbrew stout or ale
- 4 tbsp all purpose flour
- 2 tbsp olive oil
- 1/4 cup 35% cream
- 4 tbsp freshly chopped sage leaves

Preheat oven to 375°F. Cut the chicken into 8 equal size pieces, bone in, to yield the following: 2 thighs; 2 drumsticks; 2 breast tips; 2 breast base with wingette. Reserve neck and backbone for a stock. *

Roll the chicken pieces in flour seasoned with salt and pepper. In a large braising style frying pan (with tight fitting lid) heat the olive oil. Sauté the chicken pieces skin side down first, until seared golden brown.

WOMEN to WOMEN
A Gift of Hope

Remove chicken and set aside. Add leeks, garlic, mushrooms and bacon to pan, season with salt and pepper, lower heat to prevent browning. When leeks are translucent, add a bit of the beer to deglaze the pan. Stir with a wooden spoon to avoid any lumps caused by the flour on the bottom of the pan. Add the remaining beer, bring the mixture to a simmer, add chicken, cover and place in oven for approximately 35 minutes.

Check the legs of chicken with a knife to make sure the juices run clear. If it is properly cooked, remove the pan from the oven. Take the chicken out of the pan, place the pan on top of the stove at a simmer.

In a separate small saucepan, combine 2 tbsp of chicken fat skimmed from the top of the sauce with remaining flour and mix well. Add about 1/2 cup of the sauce to this and mix again. Pour all of this slurry into the sauce and mix well.

Add chopped sage and cream to sauce. Simmer for about 5 minutes to cook out any starchy flavour. Taste for seasoning (adjust with salt and pepper as necessary), add chicken to sauce, heat and serve.

Mara Jernigan

Chef/Instructor Dubrulle French Culinary School, Co-ordinator "FarmFolk/CityFolk Society" Cobble Hill, British Columbia, Canada

Coq Au Vin

"This recipe was a favourite of mine during my early married years in Vancouver, British Columbia. We lived in a tiny house in Deep Cove, looking up Indian Arm, and gave lots of dinner parties there, at the bottom of our cliffside, 30 feet from high tide."

The extra steps that make this version so good include browning the chicken and vegetables, adding brandy (flamed as it is put into the stew) and, most crucial of all, removing the finished chicken and vegetables from the sauce and reducing the sauce to about half its former quantity by a quick boil. This last intensifies the flavour of the sauce immeasurably. 'Beurre Manié' is added to make the sauce a little richer and thicken it slightly.

2 chicken breasts, halved
6 chicken legs
salt and pepper
24 medium mushrooms
24 tiny white onions
1/4 cup butter
1/4 lb thick-sliced bacon
1 tsp sugar
1 clove garlic, minced

1/4 cup brandy
2 cups dry red wine
3 cups chicken broth
1/2 tsp thyme leaves
1 bay leaf
1 tbsp fresh parsley
1 tbsp butter
1 tbsp flour

WOMEN to WOMEN
A Gift of Hope

Dry the chicken pieces thoroughly and sprinkle them with salt and pepper. Wipe off the mushrooms and remove the stems. Peel the onions. To do this effortlessly, drop them into a pot of boiling water. Count to 10 slowly (count higher for bigger onions), then drain the onions and run them under cold water. The skin will slip off between your fingers. Cut bacon into 1/2" pieces and cook in butter in a large Dutch oven or casserole until lightly browned. Remove bacon and drain. Pour half of the accumulated fat into a second large pan or skillet so you can use two pans for browning the chicken. Add the chicken to fat, skin side down, without crowding. Cook it over medium heat until lightly browned on both sides. As pieces brown, remove them and add more. When all are browned, set aside. From now on you will work only with the heavy casserole. Put the onions into it, add sugar and cook, stirring until onions are lightly browned. Then brown mushrooms and garlic. Put the chicken back in the pot and pour most of the brandy in over it. Retain about one tablespoonful and put it into a ladle. Light the brandy in the ladle and pour it, flaming, into the casserole to ignite the rest. When you do this, stand back as the whole casserole will flame up instantly. When the flame dies, add the wine, broth and herbs. Cover pan and simmer for 30 minutes or until the chicken is tender. Remove chicken, bacon, mushrooms and onions. Bring stock left in pan to a boil, skimming off fat. Boil stock rapidly for about five minutes or until liquid is reduced to about two cups. Mix one tablespoon

Hon. Barbara J. McDougall

International Strategic Advisor, Corporate Director
Toronto, Ontario, Canada

continued on next page

Coq Au Vin —*continued*

butter and flour together and stir this 'beurre
manié' into the sauce. Cook until the sauce
thickens. Strain and pour over chicken.
If you are making the 'Coq Au Vin' ahead,
strain the sauce into a separate container and
store it in the refrigerator. To reheat, place
covered chicken in 325°F oven for about
30 minutes. Arrange on platter. Meanwhile,
reheat sauce separately and pour over chicken.
Serve with rice that has been fluffed up with
butter and parsley.

Beef Kofta Curry

"This is my grandfather's famous recipe (in the Okanagan, anyway)."

2 tsp salt
2 cloves garlic, crushed
8 oz beef, minced
2 tbsp oil
4 cloves
8 single black
  pepper corns
2 pieces cinnamon sticks
2 bay leaves
1 clove brown cardamon

1 medium onion,
  chopped
2 medium sized
  tomatoes, quartered
1 tbsp yogurt
1/2 tsp red chili powder
1 1/4 cups water
1/2 tsp garam masala
1 tbsp coriander leaves,
  chopped

Judi Tyabji

*Former Politician and
Broadcaster
Producer, Maradadi Pacific
Productions
Co-founder of Progressive
Democratic Alliance
Victoria, British Columbia, Canada*

"Best of luck with your efforts."

Mix 1/2 tsp salt and garlic with the meat. Divide the mix into 12 parts, and roll each into a ball. Heat oil on moderate heat in a deep saucepan. Add chopped onions and saute. Add cloves, peppercorns, cinnamon, bay leaves and cardamons and stir thoroughly. When onion turns golden, add the tomatoes, yogurt and chili powder. Water is poured in along with remaining salt. The mix is brought to a boil. Meat balls are now dropped in and again brought to a boil. Cover the pan and allow to simmer 15 minutes or until the meat is cooked through.

Sprinkle masala and coriander and serve hot. Makes 12 meat balls.

Women to Women
A Gift of Hope

Oiseaux du Paradis

"Présentation spectaculaire pour un souper entre amis(es)."

2 poulets de
  Cornouailles
  (Game Chicken)

2 ananas frais entiers

1 chopine de
  champignons frais
  tranchés

6 c. à soupe de beurre

1 tasse de lait

1 c. à soupe de farine

2 tasses de pommes de
  terre en purée

sel, poivre

Chauffer le four à 325°F. Couper les poulets en deux. Faire revenir 3 c. à soupe de beure dans un poêlon. Faire brunir les 1/2 poulets. Les mettre dans un plat allant au four et faire cuire 45 minutes.

Durant ce temps, faire fondre le reste du beurre, y ajouter les champignons et la farine pour faire une pâte. Rajouter le lait froid peu à peu en brassant afin de faire une sauce. Réserver.

Couper les ananas sur le long en conservant les feuilles, les vider et garder la pulpe pour un dessert.

Lorsque le poulet est cuit, en mettre 1/2 par 1/2 ananas, entourer d'une couronne de pommes de terre et passer à "GRILL" une dizaine de minutes.

"Je suis très heureuse de pouvoir joindre l'utile à l'agréable pour soutenir cette cause si importante. (I am very happy to be part of this useful and pleasant endeavour in support of such an important cause.)"

WOMEN to WOMEN
A Gift of Hope

Servir dans une assiette chaude et arroser de sauce aux champignons.

Spectaculaire!

English Translation:

Birds of Paradise

"Spectacular presentation for a supper among friends."

2 cornish hens	1 cup milk
2 whole fresh pineapples	1 tbsp flour
1 lb mushrooms	2 cups mashed potatoes
6 tbsp butter	salt and pepper

Preheat oven to 325°F. Cut hens in half and brown in half the butter. Bake in oven for 45 minutes.

Melt remaining butter, add mushrooms and saute. Add flour to make a paste. Add milk and stir to make sauce.

Cut pineapple in half (lengthwise) and hollow-out. Save fruit for dessert.

Place one half cooked hen in hollowed out pineapple shell. Pipe potatoes around hen and brown under broiler. Drizzle with sauce and mushrooms.

Spectacular!

L'honorable Lucienne Robillard

Députée Fédérale de la Circonscription de Westmount-Ville-Marie, Ministre de la Citoyenneté et de L'immigration (Minister of Citizenship and Immigration and Member of Parliament, Westmount-Ville-Marie) Ottawa, Ontario, Canada

Ziggy's Spicy Pot Roast

4 to 5 lb beef pot roast

1/4 cup shortening

3 cup water

1 cup vinegar

1/2 cup brown sugar

1/2 cup chopped onion

2 tbsp mixed pickling spices

2 tsp cardamom seed

1/3 cup flour

1/3 cup cold water

In a Dutch oven or skillet, brown meat slowly on all sides in the shortening. Pour off excess fat.

Add next six ingredients. Simmer, covered, 3 to 4 hours or until meat is tender.

Remove meat and keep warm until serving.

Ziggy Lorenc

T.V. Host, "Life on Venus Ave" and "Ziggy"
Toronto, Ontario, Canada

Spicy Chicken

2 tsp curry powder

1 tsp cumin

1/2 tsp ground ginger

1/2 tsp turmeric

1/2 clove garlic, crushed

1 onion, chopped

1 tsp fresh ginger, grated

1 medium chicken,
cut into serving pieces
and skinned

Combine dry ingredients with garlic, onion and fresh grated ginger. Coat chicken with mixture and refrigerate for 2 hours, preferably longer. Place on moderately hot barbecue grill or broil in oven approximately 30 minutes or until done, turning once.

Serves 4.

Elizabeth Taylor

Actress
Bel Air, California, U.S.A.

WOMEN *to* WOMEN
A Gift of Hope

Lancashire Hotpot

"This is a traditional meal from the North of England. Although every good 'housewife' learned how to make this dish, the best I ever tasted was my Mum's. This is her recipe."

6 to 8 large lambchops (or less expensive neckchops)

flour

2 tbsp olive oil

6 medium onions, chopped

6 medium potatoes, thinly sliced

1 cup button mushrooms

salt, pepper, bay leaf

sprig of rosemary

Trim the fat off the chops and turn in the flour. Brown in hot olive oil.

Layer the sliced potatoes, mushrooms and chops in either a clay pot or a casserole dish. Add seasoning and 2 cups water. Cover. Bake in oven for 1 1/2 hours at 275 to 300°F. Remove lid and cook for an additional 1 hour at 325°F.

Finish by browning the top layer of potatoes under the grill.

Serve piping hot. Great with red cabbage.

Serves 6.

Debbie Travis

Host and Producer of "The Painted House" TV series and Author of The Painted House *and* Debbie Travis' Decorating Solutions
Westmount, Quebec, Canada

"I was 12 years old when I lost my father to cancer and 28 when my mother died of this dreadful disease. I take very seriously the raising of funds for cancer in the hope that one day a cure will be found."

WOMEN *to* WOMEN
A Gift of Hope

Chicken Oregano

"I love Italian food. As a matter of fact, I love Italians! They cook with a 'magic pot'. No matter how many unexpected guests show up for dinner, the 'magic pot' expands to feed them. That's amore!!!!"

4 boneless chicken breasts

1 stick butter

oregano

garlic powder

pepper

1/3 cup grated Parmesan cheese

2 cups mushrooms, sliced

1 box spaghetti noodles

1 tbsp Wesson oil

Jonathan Exley

Preheat oven to 375°F. Place 3 tbsp butter over chicken, sprinkle with oregano and garlic. Bake for 45 minutes to an hour. Add mushrooms for last 10 minutes of baking time.

In large pot, add oil to boiling water, cook noodles and drain.

Sprinkle 1/4 cup Parmesan cheese, oregano and pepper on bottom of platter. Place noodles on top of spices on platter. Sprinkle Parmesan cheese, oregano and pepper over noodles.

Melt 5 tbsp butter and pour over noodles.

Place chicken and mushrooms over noodles and serve.

Florence Henderson

*Singer, Actress,
Cookbook Author and
"Ultimate Mom"*
Marina del Rey, California, U.S.A.

WOMEN *to* WOMEN
A Gift of Hope

Life isn't a matter of milestones, but of moments.

Rose Kennedy

Firelight

Delicious after-dinner indulgences

WOMEN *to* WOMEN
A Gift of Hope

No Cooking Banana Pie

"This is healthy. There is no sugar, no dairy, no cooking and beautiful to look at."

Sooter's

Gladys Aaron

Author and Fitness Instructor
North York, Ontario, Canada

1/2 lb pitted dates
1/3 lb apricots, dried
3 medium bananas
1 medium banana
1 cup boiled water

1/3 cup coconut, unsweetened or 1/3 cup toasted hulled sesame seeds
plus another 1/3 cup or more of coconut to sprinkle on top of pie

Soak dates and apricots in boiled water to soften. Pour off water and save. Mix in food processor on "knife blade" adding the coconut or sesame seeds. Spread on bottom of pie plate (not too thick for less sweetness).

Slice 3 medium bananas and lay on top of spread. Blend 1 banana using a little of the soaked water (from dates) adding either a slice of papaya, peach or mango for added flavour. Pour over sliced bananas to seal. This is your cream.

Sprinkle coconut on top and decorate with whatever fruit you chose (either peaches, papaya or mango). Decorate using broccoli leaves, kiwi slices, strawberries and a flower.

Very pleasing to the eye.

If any spread is left, roll in coconut or sesame seeds and have some delightful confections.

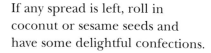

WOMEN *to* WOMEN
A Gift of Hope

Crunchy Pie

Beat 3 egg whites
    until stiff

Add 1 tsp baking powder

Fold in 1 scant *cup*
    granulated sugar

Fold in 11 single
    graham crackers
    (crushed)

Fold in 1 cup
    chopped walnuts

Put in greased pie plate and bake in 350°F oven
for 1/2 hour.

Let cool and top with whipped cream or
ice cream.

Enjoy!

Crunchy Pie is pictured on page 109.

Betty White

Actress
Los Angeles, California, U.S.A.

*"Many thanks for your help in
a good cause. All the best."*

WOMEN *to* WOMEN
A Gift of Hope

143

Fresh Strawberry Tarte

Carole Taylor

Chair,
Vancouver Port Corporation
Vancouver, British Columbia,
Canada

"This is for all my great women
friends, especially my daughter."

"I love the pure strawberry taste to this dessert, the first taste of summer. Save this recipe for a day when the strawberries are so red and so juicy that you simply cannot resist them!"

1 baked tarte shell	*1 tbsp butter*
4 cups strawberries	*red food colouring,*
1 cup sugar	*if necessary*
2 tbsp cornstarch	*4 oz cream cheese*
1/4 cup cointreau	

Wash, hull berries. Select about 25 of the best to be placed large end down on crust later. Purée remaining berries (about 1 1/2 cups). Place purée in saucepan, bring to boil, add sugar.

Mix cornstarch with liqueur and add to purée. Allow to simmer until thick and clear. Stir frequently to avoid sticking for about 5 to 8 minutes. Remove from heat and add colouring, if necessary.

Place cream cheese and about 1 tbsp purée in cuisenart. Blend until smooth, in bursts. Spread over tarte shell. Arrange berries with largest at centre in concentric circles. Pour glaze over berries, covering all evenly. When somewhat cool, place in fridge.

This tarte takes time to set and cuts best the next day. Serve with whipping cream or ice cream.

WOMEN *to* WOMEN
A Gift of Hope

Fresh Strawberry Tarte is pictured on page 110.

Strawberry Rhubarb Dessert

4 cups rhubarb

1 cup water

1 pkg strawberry Jell-O

1 cup sugar

1 pkg plain white cake mix

Mix rhubarb, water, Jell-O and sugar in bottom of a pan.

Sprinkle the cake mix over mixture and pat on top.

Melt 1/2 cup of butter and pour on top and bake at 350°F oven for 30 to 40 minutes.

Jane Barry

Solicitor General, Government of New Brunswick
Saint John, New Brunswick, Canada

"I am honoured to be part of this worthwhile project."

Blueberry Grunt

"This is my children's favourite as it was my favourite growing up as a child. I have no idea whether the recipe was an original of my mother's or whether it was handed down from her mother. I do know that it is not in any of my mother's cookbooks so I give it to you with deep appreciation of the work that you are doing."

4 cups frozen or   1/2 cup sugar or
     fresh blueberries   substitute sugar

Place in a casserole dish at 350°F and allow to bubble.

Meanwhile, make your favourite tea biscuit recipe or if in a rush, use a commercial tea biscuit package.

Make sure your biscuits are about 1 1/2" in diameter and drop on top of the bubbling berries.

Increase the oven temperature to 450°F. Cook until biscuits are beginning to brown, usually about 10 minutes.

Serve with whipping cream.

Michael Bedford Photography

Hon. Sharon Carstairs

Senator
Ottawa, Ontario, Canada

Plum Torte

"Dedicated to my mother, a breast cancer survivor. This is a great aprés-ski recipe. If you run into a friend while skiing and they invite you for an impromptu dinner, you can still ski until 4 p.m., whip this torte together by 6 p.m. and impress the heck out of them!"

1/2 cup unsalted butter	pinch of salt
3/4 cup sugar	2 eggs
1 cup unbleached flour, sifted	12 purple plums
1 tsp baking powder	lemon juice and cinnamon for topping

Preheat oven to 350°F. Cream butter and 1/2 cup sugar. Add flour, baking powder, salt, eggs and beat well.

Put into spring form 8" or 9" pan. Cut plums in half, remove pits, place plum halves on top, skin side down. Sprinkle with remaining sugar (1/4 cup) and cinnamon, lemon juice.

Bake 1 hour.

Instead of plums, you can use blueberries or peaches or apples or you can use more than 1 fruit in combination.

Top torte with whipped cream. Best made with real whipping cream and 1 tsp of sugar and beaten with electric beater (until stiff) just before serving.

Pamela Martin

Television News Anchor, BCTV; Chairperson of Canadian Cancer Society of B.C./Yukon
Vancouver, British Columbia, Canada

"We are winning this fight, together as women, and I'm convinced we will soon conquer it, especially with efforts like this book!"

WOMEN to WOMEN
A Gift of Hope

Corn Pudding

"This is my favourite because it was passed down to me from my mother who got it from my grandmother. It is very special."

1 can of cream style corn

1 can of whole kernel corn (drained)

3 eggs

1 stick of butter (broken into pieces)

4 tbsp sugar

1 tsp flour

1/2 cup milk

dash of nutmeg

Mix the corn, butter, sugar, and flour in a bowl. Beat the eggs with a fork until frothy before adding to mixture. Add milk. Stir well.

Place ingredients in a baking dish. Sprinkle nutmeg on top.

Bake at 375°F uncovered, until golden brown. Serve while hot.

Makes 4 to 6 servings.

Dr. Janet Taylor

Psychiatrist
West Vancouver, British Columbia, Canada

"Sojourner Truth said 'It is the mind that makes the body.' As women we must educate ourselves about the physical and spiritual aspects of being women that make us special and strong in order to maintain them."

WOMEN *to* WOMEN
A Gift of Hope

Dolly Parton's Banana Pudding

"This special dessert is Dolly's treat at Aunt Granny's Restaurant in 'Dollywood'."

2 12oz boxes vanilla wafers ("Nilla wafers)

3 pounds bananas, sliced

1 1/2 cups sugar

1/2 cup all purpose flour

6 egg yolks

3 whole eggs

1/2 cup butter

dash salt

6 cups milk

2 tsp vanilla

Layer sliced bananas and vanilla wafers in large baking pan. Mix together sugar, flour, eggs, butter and salt in heavy-bottomed saucepan. Add the milk, a little at a time. Cook slowly until the mixture thickens. Let it cool for a few minutes, then add the vanilla. Pour over bananas and vanilla wafers.

Meringue topping

6 egg whites

1 tsp lemon juice

1 tsp sugar

1 tsp vanilla

Beat the egg whites with lemon juice, sugar and vanilla until stiff. Spoon this mixture over the top of the pudding and brown at 350°F for 10 to 12 minutes or until golden on top.

Makes 10 to 12 servings.

Dolly Parton

Singer, Songwriter, Actress
Brentwood, Tennessee, U.S.A.

"Wishing you much success."

WOMEN to WOMEN
A Gift of Hope

149

БЛИНЧИКИ СО СЛИВКАМИ

1/2 л. молока
200 -230 гр. пшеничной муки (в зависимости от влажности)
2 яйца
1 ч.л. соли
1 ст.л. сахара
1/2 ч.л. рыхлителя или пищевой соды
4 ст.л. кукурузного масла

В теплое молоко добавить соль, сахар, взбитые яйца, масло, рыхлитель или пищевую соду и все смешать. Продолжая взбивать, добавить просеянную муку. Если окажутся комки, то процедить через сито. Дать постоять массе 20 минут.

Затем выпекать блины (толщиной около 2 мм) с двух сторон на горячей сковородке с тефлоновым покрытием. Блины сложить в форму (по размеру блина - около 20 см), поливая каждый блин 4-5 ст.л. сливок (20 % жирности). Закрыть форму крышкой или фольгой и в течении 30 минут запекать в духовом шкафу при температуре 200⁰С.

Готовые блины разрезать на сегменты и подавать к столу горячими.

Надеюсь, что мои блинчики Вам понравятся.

Editors' note:
Original recipe submitted by Naina Yeltsina.

WOMEN to WOMEN
A Gift of Hope

English Translation:

Cream Layer Crepes

"I hope you like my crepes."

2 cups milk

3/4 cup (approximately) all purpose flour

2 eggs

cream (20%)

1 tsp salt

1 tbsp sugar

1/2 tsp baking soda

4 tbsp corn oil

Warm the milk and add salt, sugar, beaten eggs, corn oil and baking soda. Mix everything well. While beating mixture, add sifted flour. If mixture get lumpy, sift it through a sieve. Let stand 20 minutes.

Bake crepes (1/4" thick) on both sides in a hot Teflon-coated frying pan. Stack all the crepes into a dish the same size as the crepes, spreading 4 to 5 tbsp of cream (20% fat) on each crepe.

Cover the dish containing the crepes with its lid or aluminum foil and bake in the oven at 400°F for 30 minutes. When crepes are ready, cut them in wedges and serve hot.

Naina Yeltsina

Wife of the Russian President Boris Yeltsin
Moscow, Russia

WOMEN *to* WOMEN
A Gift of Hope

151

The Working Girl's Dream

"This recipe belonged to a very dear friend, Joy Allchurch, who died of cancer many years ago before there was much hope. It's delicious, guests love it and it's easy to make."

22 Jatz (Ritz) biscuits
3 egg whites
1 cup chopped pecan nuts
1 tsp vanilla
1 cup whipped cream
shaved sweet chocolate

Crumb 22 biscuits very finely by placing between 2 tea towels and crushing with a rolling pin (or use food processor).

Beat egg whites until stiff. Gradually add sugar, continuing to beat until well mixed. Add crumbed biscuits, pecans and vanilla. Fold in carefully.

Place mixture in a greased pie plate and bake at 350°F for 20 to 24 minutes.

Cool and top with 1 cup of whipping cream. Shave sweet chocolate on top and chill in refrigerator until ready to serve.

Leneen Forde, A.C.

Former State Governor Queensland Australia; Lawyer; Past International President Zonta
Bilinga, Queensland, Australia

"As I was born and lived in Ottawa (Canada) until I was 19, I was very pleased to be asked to support your endeavours to help battle breast cancer by heightening awareness and raising funds for research."

152

WOMEN to WOMEN
A Gift of Hope

Applesauce for Dessert

For each person use

*1 good apple, cored
and cut into about
20 pieces, leaving
skin on*

*and 1 or 2 pieces of
lemon peel*

Put in heavy pot with a lid, cook on lowest flame possible until apples get mushy, 10 or 15 minutes (can be done with higher heat if in a hurry).

When apples are mushy, mash to a pulp (lemon peel can be left in for more flavour) with potato masher, add one packet Equal or Sweet 'N Low.

While still warm, put in crystal dessert dish and top with 1/2 carton plain yogurt sweetened with 1 packet Sweet 'N Low or Equal. Dust nutmeg on top.

Helen Gurley Brown

Editor-In-Chief,
Cosmopolitan *International Editions*
New York, New York, U.S.A.

*"Anything that helps breast
cancer detection and cure is
a wonderful and worthy cause."*

J.M. Carisse Photo

Hon. Hedy Fry, P.C., MP

Secretary of State,
Multiculturalism and
Status of Women
Hull, Quebec, Canada

"I am honoured to be a part of
the Celebrity Lights II *project.*
As Secretary of State (Status of
Women) and as a physician,
I realize the importance of our joint
efforts to raise awareness of and
eradicate this horrible disease."

Hazelnut Cake

"This has been a family favourite for years.
Absolutely delicious and simple to create."

2 tbsp sifted flour	3/4 cup sugar
2 1/2 tsp baking powder	1 cup hazelnuts
4 eggs	

Heat oven to 350°F. Grease two 8" cake pans,
line with wax paper and grease again. Sift flour
and baking powder and set aside. Put eggs and
sugar into blender container, cover and process
at "Mix." When smooth, remove feeder cap and
add hazelnuts. Continue processing until flour is
well mixed. Pour batter into prepared pans and
bake for 20 minutes or until cake tester comes
out clean. Invert pans and cool. Remove from
pans; sift powdered sugar over top of layers or
top with mocha whipped cream.

WOMEN *to* WOMEN
A Gift of Hope

Perfect Pumpkin Cheesecake

Crust

1 3/4 cups crushed
   ginger snaps

1/2 cup melted
   margarine (or butter)

Bake at 350°F for 15 minutes in spring-form pan.
Let cool before filling.

Filling

2 packages cream cheese

3/4 cup sugar

3/4 cup sour cream

1 can pumpkin (14 oz)

1 tsp nutmeg

1 tsp cinnamon

1 tsp vanilla

2 tbsp dark rum
   (optional)

Cream ingredients. Pour onto ginger snap crust.
Bake for 1 1/2 hours at 350°F. Let cool.
Sprinkle with sugar and cinnamon. Top with
whipped cream.

Topping

2 tsp sugar

1 tsp cinnamon

whipped cream

Meribeth Burton

Host of
"CHEK News at 5:00"
Victoria, British Columbia, Canada

WOMEN *to* WOMEN
A Gift of Hope

Auntie Judy's Healthy Scoop Ginger Ice Cream

*4 cups undiluted
evaporated milk*

1 1/2 cups 35% cream

4 large eggs

1 packet gelatin

ginger syrup (see below)

Soften gelatin according to manufacturer's instructions. In the meantime, in a heavy saucepan, heat the evaporated milk (do not scald or boil). Whisk the softened gelatin into the milk.

In another bowl, whisk the egg yolk. Whisk the 35% cream into the egg yolk. Add egg yolk and cream mixture into the milk and gelatin mixture. Blend in the ginger syrup. Churn on an ice-cream freezer according to manufacturer's instructions. To serve, top with slivers of candied ginger or crushed roasted peanuts or pistachios. Enjoy!

Ginger syrup

1/2 lb fresh ginger root	1 cup white sugar
2 cups water	juice of 1 lemon

Dice ginger root and blend in blender with the water, add the lemon juice.

In a heavy saucepan, bring the ginger mixture to a boil, simmer for 10 minutes and let cool. When cool, strain the ginger mixture through a sieve until much of the liquid is extracted. Discard solids.

In a heavy saucepan, combine the ginger liquid with 1 cup white sugar. Bring mixture to a boil and simmer for 10 minutes. Set aside to cool.

Suzanne Boyd

Editor-In-Chief of
Flare *Magazine*
Toronto, Ontario, Canada

"I am very excited about this project."

Spa Chocolate Mousse

"Rich, decadent chocolate without an ounce of guilt. Sufficiently satisfies the cravings we all get now and then!"

1 3/4 tsp gelatin powder

1 egg yolk

2 egg whites

1/2 cup unsweetened cocoa powder

3/4 cup sugar

1 1/4 cups evaporated skim milk

1 tsp vanilla

pinch cream of tartar

2 oz unsweetened chocolate

Sprinkle gelatin over 1/4 cup of cold water in a small cup. Let stand, without stirring, for at least 5 minutes or until needed.

Place the egg yolk in a cup beside the stove and have ready a small whisk. Combine the cocoa with 1/3 cup of sugar in a small saucepan. Stir in enough milk to form a paste. Stir in the remaining milk. Bring mixture to a simmer over medium heat, stirring frequently with a wooden spoon. Simmer gently for about 2 minutes. Remove from the heat and whisk a small amount of the hot mixture into the egg yolk. Scrape the mixture back into the pot and whisk well to combine. It will be hot enough to be safe. It will thicken without further cooking.

WOMEN to WOMEN
A Gift of Hope

Stir in the softened gelatin, chopped chocolate and vanilla. Let stand a minute and whisk again until the chocolate has completely melted and the mixture is perfectly smooth.

Set the saucepan in a large bowl of ice water to cool and thicken. Stir and scrape the sides from time to time. If mixture begins to set before needed, remove from the ice bath, whisk and set aside.

To make the meringue, bring 2" of water to a boil in a large saucepan. Combine the cream of tartar and 2 teaspoons of water in a 4-to-6-cup stainless steel bowl. Whisk in the egg whites and 1/2 cup of sugar. Set the bowl in the saucepan. Stir the mixture briskly and constantly with a whisk or rubber spatula for about 1 minute. Remove the bowl from the saucepan and insert a thermometer; the temperature must be at least 160°F. When the bowl is removed, beat the egg whites on high speed until cool and stiff.

Fold about a quarter of the cooled chocolate mixture into the beaten egg whites. Scrape the egg white mixture back into the remaining chocolate mixture. Fold to combine. Scrape mixture into dessert glasses, cover and refrigerate for at least 2 hours or until set. Mousse may be refrigerated, covered.

Garnish with 1/2 a strawberry, 2 raspberries and/or a mint leaf.

Serves 10.

Wendy Lisogar-Cocchia

President, Spa at the Century and Executive Vice President of Century Plaza Hotel and Spa Group
Vancouver, British Columbia, Canada

"We can't redirect the winds but we can adjust the sails. Life is truly too short not to enjoy every bit of it. Be a kind person, and definitely do not sweat the small stuff. Have fun each and every day and eat lots of chocolate!"

Bittersweet-Chocolate Cheesecake

"Let them eat cake! You won't believe it's low fat!"

Instead of high-fat cream cheese, this low-fat version is made with yogurt cheese (see below), yet the cake tastes rich and creamy. The yogurt plays wonderfully off the bittersweet chocolate.

1 tbsp butter, melted

1/4 cup chocolate
    wafer crumbs

1/2 cup brown sugar

1 cup granulated sugar

3/4 cup cocoa powder

1/2 cup all purpose
    flour

1/4 tsp salt

1/2 cup chocolate or
    Irish cream liqueur

2 tsp vanilla extract

2 eggs

2 oz (or 2 squares)
    bittersweet chocolate,
    melted

about 3 cups
    yogurt cheese

Garnish

1/2 cup white chocolate shavings

Preheat oven to 300°F. Put a bowl of water on the lower rack. Brush sides and bottom of an 8" spring form pan with melted butter. Sprinkle chocolate wafer crumbs evenly over bottom of pan. Set aside.

In a bowl, mix together sugars, cocoa powder, flour and salt. Set aside.

Put liqueur, vanilla, eggs, melted chocolate and yogurt cheese in food processor. Begin processing and gradually pour in dry ingredients. Process until just combined. Do not overmix or yogurt cheese will liquefy. Pour yogurt mixture over crumbs in the pan. Bake 1 1/4 hours on the middle rack of oven. Cool completely, run a knife around outside of cake; chill for 2 hours. Remove outside of pan and garnish with white chocolate.

Serves 8 to 10.

Yogurt Cheese

Yogurt cheese, essentially yogurt drained of much of its water, is the consistency of soft cream cheese.

6 cups plain 2% yogurt
  (make sure it does not contain gelatin,
  which appears on some labels as pectin)

Drain yogurt by placing in a fine-mesh sieve positioned on the rim of a bowl. Cover yogurt with plastic wrap and refrigerate for 8 hours. Pour off the water collected after 2 hours to keep the water level down. After 8 hours of draining, there should be about 3 cups of cheese. Discard water.

Cobi Ladner

Magazine Editor,
Canadian House and Home
Toronto, Ontario, Canada

161

This is the song that never ends,

It just goes on and on my friends...

Somebody started singing it, not knowing what it was,

And we'll just keep on singing it forever, just because...

Shining Light

A Tribute to Shari Lewis

WOMEN *to* WOMEN
A Gift of Hope

Shari Lewis' Mozzarella Marinara

Before her passing, Shari expressed her wish to share in the gift of hope and chose one of her favourite recipes for inclusion in the *Celebrity Lights II* Cookbook. This was her selection...

16 oz mozzarella cheese in 1/2" slices

1/2 cup flour

2 eggs, slightly beaten

1 cup herbed, seasoned bread crumbs

olive oil

1 can (10 1/2 oz) pizza sauce

1 can (2 oz) flat anchovies

Dip cheese into egg, flour and back into egg (moisten all surfaces). Pack bread crumbs against cheese and place on a plate in freezer for 20 minutes. Pour 1/4" of oil in a frying pan. When very hot, add cold cheese slices and brown both sides crisply. Drain on a paper towel.

To serve, top with warmed sauce, and an anchovy strip.

Dana Fineman/Sygma

Shari Lewis

Children's Entertainer, Ventriloquist, Puppeteer, Singer and Author, best known for her work with the lovable puppet, Lamb Chop.

Shari Lewis, who passed away on August 2nd, 1998, was – and will continue to be – a shining light to children all over the world.

I've always believed that one woman's success can only help another woman's success

Gloria Vanderbilt

Guiding Light

The Celebrity Lights Production Team

WOMEN *to* WOMEN
A Gift of Hope

The Ultimate Nanaimo Bar Recipe

Several years ago, the Mayor of the City of Nanaimo conducted a search to find the ultimate Nanaimo Bar Recipe. Since the Celebrity Lights project also originated in Nanaimo, the Production Team thought it was fitting to share those results. Here it is... to munch, savour and enjoy. Smooth, scrumptious and delectable! This recipe is credited to Joyce Hardcastle.

Bottom Layer

1/2 cup unsalted butter (European style cultured)

1/4 cup sugar

5 tbsp cocoa

1 egg, beaten

1 3/4 cups graham wafer crumbs

1/2 cup finely chopped almonds

1 cup coconut

Melt first three ingredients in top of double boiler. Add egg and stir to cook and thicken. Remove from heat. Stir in crumbs, coconut and nuts. Press firmly into an ungreased 8 x 8" pan.

Terry Patterson

Second Layer

1/2 cup unsalted butter

2 tbsp and 2 tsp cream

2 tbsp vanilla custard powder

2 cups icing sugar

Cream butter, cream, custard powder and icing sugar together well. Beat until light. Spread over bottom layer.

Third Layer

4 squares semi-sweet chocolate (1 oz each)

2 tbsp unsalted butter

Melt chocolate and butter over low heat. Cool. When cool, but still liquid, pour over second layer and chill in refrigerator.

The Celebrity Lights Production Team

Nanaimo, British Columbia, Canada

Back Row (left to right):
Shelley Anderson,
Michelle Krall, Valerie Luedke,
Deborah Melanson, Carrie Crowe
Front Row (left to right):
Kim Stallknecht,
Adella Krall, Karen Mason,
Donna Dash, Lynn Krynowsky,
Jessica Melanson, Cora Wilson

The richness of the human experience would lose
something of rewarding joy
if there were no limitations to overcome.

Helen Keller

The Project

Acknowledgements, indexes and ordering details

Women to Women
A Gift of Hope

Many Thanks

Individual Contributors

The Celebrity Lights fundraising initiative has been the product of the talents, hard work and support of many people. Since its inception, literally hundreds have helped by sharing in the gift of hope. A heartfelt **Thank you** to you all for your wonderful gifts to this project.

Gladys Aaron

Taylor Adams

Ellen Addison

Bob Adshead

Gerhard Aichelberger

Trudy Alexander

Chris Allicock

Debbie Altow

Barbara Amster

Gillian Anderson

Heather Anderson

Shelley Anderson

Billy Andrusco

Catherine Armstrong

Sally Armstrong

Dr. Mary-Wynne Ashford

Margaret Atwood

Bev Bain

Barb Baird

Elizabeth Baird

Carroll Baker

Barbara Barde

Pat Barfoot

Jane Barry

Peter Battistoni

Marilyn Beck

The Best of Bridge Women

Susan Black

Renee Blackstone

Bonnie Blair

Hon. Ethel Blondin-Andrew

Suzanne Boyd

Elizabeth Bradford
  Holbrook

Lorne Braithwaite

Karen Brimacombe

Ray Brittain

Nicole Brossard

Denise Brown

Helen Gurley Brown

Rosemary Brown

Nicole Brugger

Pam Bryson

Nina Budman

Janice Burns

Meribeth Burton

Barbara Bush

Sharon Butala

Brenda Cairns

Cherie M. Calbom

June Callwood

Hon. Iona (Hardy)
  Campagnola

The Rt. Hon. Kim Campbell

Pat Carney

Ruth Carrier

Michael Carroll

Samantha Carruthers

Sharon Carstairs

Rosalyn Carter

Carolyn Chase

Liz Chase

Shelley Chase

Wei Chen

Brian Chatwin

Aline Chrétien

Coleen Christie

Peter Christle

Adrienne Clarkson

Beverly Cleary

Diane Clement

Polly Clingerman

Hillary Clinton

Tom Cochrane

Diane Nusgart Cohen

Holly Cole

Joan Collins

Kelly Collins

Nadia Comaneci

Patricia Conroy

Ken Cooke

Hon. Anne C. Cools

Hon. Sheila Copps

Hon. Nellie Cournoyea

Geri Cox

Wayne Cox

Sara Craig

Charmaine Crooks

Carrie Crowe

Jena Culley

Kelly Cunningham

Christine Curtis

Faye Dance

Barry Dash

Donna Dash

Hillary Dash

Ron Dash

Ted Dash

Robert Dees

Phyllis Diller

Sandra Dorman

Kim Douglas

Michael Downs

Anne-Marie Dryden
 Bischoff

Christiane Dryden

Leah Du Fresne, In Memory

Sandy Dulmadge

Brian Dunn

Chris Dunn

David Earl

Dorothy Earl

Lindy Edgett

Erica Ehm

Tracy Eloson

Hon. Joyce Fairbairn

Mary Lou Fassel

Dr. Sylvia Fedoruk

Don Fender

Gail Feser

Iola Feser

Keith Feser

Laura Feser

Perry Feser

Frances Fisher

Jennifer Fisher

Betty Ford

Delores Ford

Leneen Forde

Josie Forrest

Judith Forst

Margot Franssen

Sylvie Fréchette

Hon. Hedy Fry

Annette Funicello

Vicki Gabereau

Debbie Ganske

Thomas Gemma

Sandra Gillians

Rita Gobin

Bruce Gordon

Mary Halpen

Sharon Hampson

Marjorie Harris

Jane Hawtin

Florence Henderson

Pauline Hill

Joanne Hogan

Deborah Hope

Isabel Huggan

Monica Hughes

Valerie Hunt

Jane Hutchins

Linda Jacobsen

Susanne Jakobson

Jacki Ralph Jamieson

Steve Jenkinson

Ingrid Jensen

Mara Jernigan

Mary-Jane Jessen

Diana Johnson

Lady Bird Johnson

Jeanne Jones

Shirley Jones

Annabelle Jones-Litton

Tonja Joyce

Karen Kain

Cynthia Kasem

Joanne Kates

Mary Kay Ash

Joyce Kellet

Geraldine Kenney-Wallace

Diana Kershaw

Elsie Kershaw

Frank Kershaw

Chris Kindratsky

Bonnie Kitto

Bob Klemenchuk

Brent Knelson

Kent Knelson

Adella Krall

Diana Krall

Jim Krall

Michelle Krall

Don Kraushar

Jill Krop

Bernie Krynowsky

Lynn Krynowsky

Cobi Ladner

Karen Lange

Nigel Lark

Vicki Lawrence Schultz

Lisa Leighton

Janet Lewis

Shari Lewis

Christine Lippa

Wendy Lisogar-Cocchia

Ziggy Lorenc

Peter Luedke

Valerie Luedke

Veronica Luedke

Wilf Luedke

Pat Lumsden

Linda Lundström

Fiona MacDonald

Hon. Flora MacDonald

Jean MacDonald

Gayle MacKay

Lee Mackenzie

Janice MacKinnon

Shirley MacLaine

Natalie MacMaster

Rita MacNeil

Hon. Joy MacPhail

Shawney McCutcheon

Charles McDiarmid

Hon. Alexa McDonough

Barbara J. McDougall

John McGeachy

Morley McKeachie

Shelley McKeachie

Loreena McKennitt

Sarah McLachlan

Hon. Audrey McLaughlin

Cathy McLellan

Lyn McLeod

Sarah McNaughton

Shirley McQueen

Colin McTaggart

Cathy Madill

Joy Malbon

Jason Manning

Nancy Marino

Pamela Martin

John Mason

Karen Mason

Rona Maynard

Kathy Mattea

Judith Maxwell

Deborah Melanson

Shirley Mesbur

Joy Metcalfe

Helen Miles

Garry Miller

Vicky Miller

Jack Milliken

Barbara Mills

Hayley Mills

Camille Moffat

Lorraine Monk

Eloise Morrison

Mila Mulroney

Anne Murray

Susan Musgrave

Dr. Helen K. Mussallem

Elaine Mylett

Donna Nebenzahl

Sheila Nelson

Maeve O'Byrne

Michael James O'Connor

Evelyn O'Rourke

Nancy Page

Marlene Palmer

Dolly Parton

Jean Paré

Dale Partridge

Jody L. Paterson

Patricia Patkau

Pat Patten

Terry Patterson

Deni Pavan

Francine Pelletier

Jane Penner

Cassandra Peterson

Anne Petrie

Dini Petty

Marcia Pike

Mary Francis Pratt

Lynne Prevette

Valerie Pringle

Joelle Rabu

Susan Raduy

Heather Rankin

Rose Reisman

Glenda Reynolds

Traci Reynolds

Sandie Rinaldo

Susan Rind

Barry Ringstead

Mel Rivet

David Roach

Bonnie Robertson

Hon. Lucienne Robillard

Val Robinson

Peter Robson

Wendy Robson

Shelagh Rogers

Jennifer Rollison

Hugh Rose

Monda Rosenberg

Marg Ruttan

Vicki Ryall

Marnie Ryder

Buffy Sainte-Marie

John Salus

Donna Saugstad

Darlene Schmidt

Regina Schrambling

Sally Scott
Nola Sedgewick
Connie Sellecca
Barbara Selles
Carol Shields
Sandra Shinnan
Carrie Shoen
Jane Siberry
Chief Christine Silverberg
Luc Simard
Judy Simpson
David Smith
Linda Smith
Lucy Smith
Sonja Smits
Margaret A. Somerville
Tina Srebotnjak
Erik Stallknecht
Kim Stallknecht
Corinne Stewart
Doreen Stinson
Sandra Stone
Teresa Stratas
Carole Taylor
Elizabeth Taylor

Joanne Taylor
Lee Taylor
Sue Taylor
Marlo Thomas
Amanda Thompson
Brenda Thompson
Beverly Topping
Roberta Tower
Debbie Travis
C.J. Tripp
Mary Turner
Judy Tyabji
Janice Ungaro
Merv Unger
Jane Urquhart
Ellen Vaillencourt
Lorna Vander Haeghe
Arla Vander Voet
Claire Vermette
Carolyn Waldo
Pamela Wallin
Barbara Walters
Cecilia Walters
Lisa Walters
Sela Ward

Kim Warner
Jack Weiser
Karen Welds
Hon. Hilary M. Weston
Anne Wheeler
Betty White
Vanna White
Bob Wicklow
Marilyn Wicklow
Wendy Williams
Betty Wilson
Edward Wilson
Joan Wilson
Hon. Elizabeth Witmer
Oprah Winfrey
Katarina Witt
Katherine Woodhouse
Wendy Woodley
Joanne Woodward
Colette Wright
Michelle Wright
Kristi Yamaguchi
Naina Yeltsina

Corporate Sponsors

Special thanks to the following for their generous gifts and the extra support they provided to make this project possible.

Around the World Travel

Baxter Air

The Bay

Bestwick & Partners Chartered Accountants

Budget Mini-Storage

Canada Post

Canadian Airlines

Canadian Cancer Society

Central Island Broadcasting

CHEK TV

Coast Bastion Inn

Dash-Anderson Marketing Group

Essence Magazine

First Strike Consulting

Fleming Printing Ltd.

Form Consultants

Friesens Book Division

Harbour City Star

Impact Graphis

Island Paper Mills Co. Ltd.

S. J. Krall C.A. Ltd.

Kwik Kopy Printing

McMillan College – The Training Centre

Mystical Wizard Candle Co.

Nanaimo Daily News

Nanaimo News Bulletin

Neo Graphic Communications

Overwaitea Foods

Terry Patterson Photography

Piccadilly Promotions

Purolator

Quadra Printers Ltd.

Royal Bank of Canada

SJD Home Fashions

Kim Stallknecht Photography

The Wickaninnish Inn

Cora Wilson & Associates, Lawyers

Zonta Club of Nanaimo

Other Supporting Businesses

We also thank the many retailers and businesses who have supported the *Celebrity Lights* project by purchasing and/or selling books without profit.

A & W Restaurant – Tillicum Mall

Alberni Mall

Anna's Hair Design

A Step Ahead Footwear Inc.

Bank of Montreal

Bank of Nova Scotia

Bargains Galore

The Bay

Beachcomber Hair Salon

Bead Street

Bestwick & Partners

Bolen Books

Bountiful Books

Broughton Square Postal Outlet & Lottery

Cambridge Shopping Centres Ltd.

Can West Shopping Centre

Canadian Imperial Bank of Commerce

Carmel by the Sea

Chatwin Engineering Ltd.

Chemainus Books

Christensen Mazda

Coast Country Insurance

Coast Hospitality Inn

Comox Centre Mall

Comox Valley Flowers

Compucentre – Nanaimo

Cotton Ginny Plus

Country Club Centre

Country Grocer

Crabtree & Evelyn

Demie's Shoes

Driftwood Mall

Earth Easy

Eaton's

Entrée Lifestyles

Esquimalt Plaza Merchants Association

Estetia

Eurodown Quilts

Evans Bastion Insurance Agencies Ltd.

Faces & Shear Design

Fairway Market

Fanny's Fabrics & Home Accents

Flandangles

Fraser & Naylor

The Fringe & Tassel

Gallery Plus

Georgia Strait Outfitters

Getting It Write Cards – Gifts – Filofax

Gnomes Kitchens

Hair Razors Salon

Happy Hands Crafts & Gifts

Harbour Park Mall

Hemlock Printers Ltd.

Hillside Centre

His 'n' Hers Jewellers

Ironwood Mall

Island Custom Message Centre

Ivy's Bookshop

Jewelry International

J.T. Flair Salon

Just Right Gifts

Kilmary Lodge

Ladies Only Fitness

Lavender & Lace

Levesque Securities Inc. –
    Ruby Diamond, CFP

The Levi's Store

London Optical

Looking Glass Books

McConnon, Bion, O'Connor & Peterson

McMillan College Inc.,
    The Training Centre

Market Square

Marks & Spencer

Marlin Travel – Mayfair Shopping Centre

Marlin Travel – Woodgrove Centre

Marshall Ford

Mayfair Shopping Centre

McLean's Specialty Foods

Medichair Medical Equipment

Mercia's

Merle Norman

Morguard Investments Limited

Mulberry Book Store

Nanaimo Breast Screening Clinic

Nanaimo Chamber of Commerce

Nanaimo Chrysler

Nanaimo Nissan

Nanaimo Honda Cars

Nanaimo Realty

The Newsrack

Odlum Brown Limited

Overwaitea

Pacific Coast Savings Credit Union

Pampered Chef

The Panhandler

Pastel's Café

Pennington's Wearhouse

Peoples Drug Mart

Pharmasave Ltd.

Planet Hollywood

Port Alberni Chamber of Commerce

Ramars Gifts, Bradford Collectibles

Regis

J. Rounis & Co.

Royal Bank of Canada

Rutherford Mall

Sassafras – Mayfair Shopping Centre

Save-on Foods

Sawyer's Sewing Centre

Scizzorhandz

The Smart Book Shop

Spaceworks

Split Ends Salon

Stephanies Children's Fashions

Sutton Group Future Realty – Walt Burgess

Tabi International

Theatre One

Thomas Cook Travel

Thunderbird Mall

Tom Harris Chev-Geo-Oldsmobille Cadillac

Toronto Real Estate Board

Toronto-DominionBank

Town & Country Realty & Insurance

Town & Country Shopping Centre

Trendy Classics Ladies' Designer Fashions

Unique Gifts & Engraving Ltd.

Vice Versa Translation

Victoria Centre Screening Mammography
    Program of B.C.

Victoria Silk 'n Lace Inc.

Villager Men's Wear

Visions One Hour Optical Ltd.

Volume One Bookstore

Watchword Editorial Services

Wembley Books & Lotto

Wembley Mall

Wesley Street Restaurant

What's Cooking

Wheaton Pontiac Buick GMC

C.D. Wilson & Associates

The Wise Owl

Woodgrove Centre

Woodgrove Knife Shoppe Ltd.

Woolly Gift Shoppe

Work World #101

Special thanks to SJD Home Fashions of Nanaimo, for supplying china, cutlery, serving dishes and accessories for the *Celebrity Lights II* photographs. Thanks also to Hazelwood Herb Farm for supplying the garnish for the food dishes.

Reprint Acknowledgements

Every effort has been made to determine the ownership of all recipes from previously published sources submitted to the *Celebrity Lights II* project, and to secure the necessary reprint permissions. In the event that an error or omission has been made, the publisher and production team warrant that it has been made inadvertently, and express regret, but trust that the originating author or publisher will treat its one-time use in this publication as a gift to breast cancer research.

We gratefully acknowledge the publishers and authors listed below for their kind permissions to repeat copyrighted material. All permissions were given free of charge as a gift to the *Celebrity Lights II* project.

Sally Armstrong, Easy, Creamy Scrambled Eggs
    Reprinted from *Homemaker's* 1994 "The Best of Brunch" by Jan Main

Hon. Elizabeth Witmer, Sweet and Nutty Broccoli Salad
    Reprinted from *Good Friends Cookbook*

Margaret Atwood, Calla Lillies
    Reprinted from *The Canlit Foodbook*, Totem Books, Toronto 1987

Vicki Gabereau, Puttanesca
    Reprinted from *Chef On The Run*, by Diane Clement
    (reproduced in *Cooking Without Looking*, by Vicki Gabereau,
    published by Douglas & McIntyre)

Margo Franssen, Linguine al Limone
    Reprinted from *Fare For Friends*, Key Porter Books

Diane Clement, Gin-Gingered Prawns
    Reprinted from *Fresh Chef On The Run*, by Diane Clement

Rona Maynard, New Salsa Cheeseburgers
    Reprinted from *Sizzlers*, by *Chatelaine* Food Editor, Monda Rosenberg,
    published by McClelland & Stewart

Shirley McQueen, Coulibiac of Fresh Lobster and Salmon
    Reprinted from *The Dinah's Cupboard Cookbook*, by Dinah Koo & Janice Poon,
    a Totem Book, a division of Collins Publishers, 1986, Don Mills, Ontario

Shelagh Rogers, Sea Bass in A Couscous Crust
    Reprinted from *More Heart Smart Cooking* by Bonnie Stern, published by Random House

Tina Srebotnjak, Herbed Swordfish Steaks
    Reprinted from *The Canadian Living Barbecue & Summer Foods Cookbook*

Hon. Barbara J. McDougall, Coq Au Vin
    Reprinted from *Great Dinners from Life*, Time Life Cookbooks

Gladys Aaron, No Cooking Banana Pie
    Reprinted from *Vegetarian Persuasion*

Cobi Ladner, Bittersweet Chocolate Cheesecake
    Reprinted from *Canadian House & Home*, October 1997 Issue

Photographs

All photographic images of the contributors in *Celebrity Lights II* were obtained and contributed by the celebrities or their representatives, or by the *Celebrity Lights II* production team. If identified on the photographs, photographers have been credited beside their work. If a photographer was not identified on a photograph, the publisher and production team express regret, but cannot accept responsibility for material not provided to them. We gratefully acknowledge the photographers and photography sources listed below, whose work appears as part of the *Celebrity Lights II* gift:

Michael Bedford Photography

J. M. Carisse

Evan Dion

Ric Ernst

Jonathan Exley

Calvin Fehr

Dana Fineman/Sygma

Jimmy Katz

Tim Leyes

Andrew MacNaughton

Mark Mainguy

Bob Martin

Nanaimo Daily News

Terry Patterson

Skrebneski

Sooter's

Sarah Young

Index by Celebrity

Somerville, Margaret
  Tomatoes, Boccacini and Basil, 64

Srebotnjak, Tina
  Herbed Swordfish Steaks, 126

Taylor, Carole
  Fresh Strawberry Tarte, 144

Taylor, Elizabeth
  Spicy Chicken, 137

Taylor, Janet
  Corn Pudding, 148

Thomas, Marlo
  Tabbouli Salad, 43

Topping, Beverly
  Pan Roasted Seabass with
  a Mustard Sauce, 120

Travis, Debbie
  Lancashire Hotpot, 138

Tyabji, Judy
  Beef Kofta Curry, 133

Ungaro, Janice
  Biscuits for my Doggie!, 56

Walters, Barbara
  Barbara Walters' Mother's
  Stuffed Cabbage Rolls, 90

Weston, Hilary
  Victoria Sponge Cake, 52

White, Betty
  Crunchy Pie, 143

Witmer, Elizabeth
  Sweet and Nutty Broccoli Salad, 42

Witt, Katarina
  Hungarian Chicken
  à la Schlemmertopf, 111

Winfrey, Oprah
  Oprah's Potatoes, 69

Yamaguchi, Kristi
  Pound Cake, 55

Yeltsina, Naina
  Cream Layer Crepes, 150

Additional Copies of Celebrity Lights II

Additional copies of *Celebrity Lights II* are available by mail or via the World Wide Web at http://www.ariel.bc.ca/celeb2.htm.

Please copy and complete the form, below, and return it to:

McMillan College
The Training Centre
3371 Shenton Road
Nanaimo, British Columbia
V9T 2H1 Canada

We regret that fax and phone orders cannot be accepted, but all book orders will be processed as quickly as possible. Allow four to six weeks for delivery.

• •

Celebrity Lights II *Order Form*

Copies of *Celebrity Lights II* are $18.00 each (CDN). Within North America, add $3.00 per copy for shipping and handling. Outside of North America, add $5.00 per copy for shipping and handling. Payment must be in Canadian funds. Please do not mail cash.

Name: _____

Mailing address: _____

_____

Daytime telephone: _____

Please send me _____ copies of *Celebrity Lights II*. My payment is by:

☐ cheque   ☐ money order

☐ VISA   Expiry date: _____

Credit card number: _____

Signature: _____

One Candle

A girl child at her window, prays out into the night

A candle on the ledge, a tiny point of light

She draws strength from its warmth, the healing of its glow

The stars flicker back to her, it seems as if they know

For a little light brings hope, to keep our dreams alive

There are others who are out there, under just one sky

When the night seems too dark, and you're sure that you're alone

From a spark springs a flame to safely guide you home

The girl is by a bedside, the room . . . hospital white,

Her mother pale and distant, something isn't right

As the emptiness surrounds her, she knows, she sees a glow

Cause angels carry candles, Mama has to follow

Girl child becomes a woman, with babies of her own
She prays they'll have her longer than history has shown
But she'll fight up through the darkness, to ensure a brighter day
Hope consumes a woman's heart, her flame will guide the way

It only takes one candle to turn darkness into day
But with the lights of many we'll surely find a way

Written and sung by Shelley Chase
Musical Composition by Darrin "Dill" Eck

(a song written for the launch of Celebrity Lights II)

Personal Recipe

Title: _____

Ingredients: _____

_____

_____

_____

_____

_____

_____

_____

Instructions: _____

_____

_____

_____

_____

_____

_____

_____

_____

_____

_____

_____

_____

_____

_____

_____

Personal Recipe

Title: _____

Ingredients: _____

_____

_____

_____

_____

_____

_____

_____

Instructions: _____

_____

_____

_____

_____

_____

_____

_____

_____

_____

_____

_____

If I can stop one Heart from breaking,

I shall not live in vain;

If I can ease one Life the Aching,

Or cool one pain,

Or help one fainting Robin

Unto his Nest again,

I shall not live in vain.

Emily Dickinson